Secrets Parents Should Know About Public Schools

by Terry Frith

Simon and Schuster
New York

Copyright © 1985 by G. Terry Frith
All rights reserved
including the right of reproduction
in whole or in part in any form
Published by Simon and Schuster
A Division of Simon & Schuster, Inc.
Simon & Schuster Building
Rockefeller Center
1230 Avenue of the Americas
New York, New York 10020
SIMON AND SCHUSTER and colophon are registered trademarks of
Simon & Schuster, Inc.
Designed by Karolina Harris
Manufactured in the United States of America
10 9 8 7 6 5 4 3 2 1
Library of Congress Cataloging in Publication Data

Frith, Terry.
   Secrets parents should know about public schools.

Bibliography: p.
1. Public schools—United States.   2. Elementary
schools—United States.   3. Home and school—United
States.   4. Parent-teacher relationships—United
States.   5. Volunteer workers in education—United
States.   I. Title.
LA217.F74   1985   371'.01'0973   85-14555
ISBN: 0-671-55845-5

Author's Acknowledgments

I am deeply grateful to many friends who offered moral support while I was writing this book, especially to Judy McDonald, a long-time friend and colleague whose counsel was graciously given; to Diana Daugherty, who conscientiously reviewed Chapter 6; to Kim Rhodes and Martha Davis of A.K.M. Typing Service, for giving up weekends and holidays to type, copy, and collate and for doing so in the best of spirits; and most of all to Angela Rapkin and Harry Rapkin, who lived and breathed every moment of the agony and ecstasy of writing and publishing this book. They made the good times better and the crises manageable. Angela, a published author in her own right and a nurturer by nature, absorbed my concerns as her own and offered many helpful suggestions about research.

On behalf of the many children whose lives I feel certain will be improved due to this book, I extend special thanks to Loren Smolker and Harry Hoffman, who helped to make a dream a reality.

I owe a tremendous debt to my editor, Susan Victor, who

has been profoundly patient with my impatience. Her professional skill and talent, her warm personality and enthusiasm have provided a sound basis for constant feedback. I can't imagine a better editor anywhere. She is one of a kind.

I would like to thank my copy editor, Veronica Johnson, for her consistency, persistence, insight, and devotion to the task. She is truly an artist.

I truly don't know where to begin thanking Herb Frith, my dear husband, for his endurance, kind words of encouragement, unending patience, and superb editing. This book would not have been written without his love, financial and emotional support, and cheerful sacrifice of hours upon hours of evenings and early mornings. He is an outstandingly gifted college professor and public speaker, and an exceptional human being. He brought these special qualities to the book and particularly to the last chapter. Most important, his confidence in me saw me through the bleak moments and led me to push personal boundaries never before explored.

To my dedicated colleagues, whose professional skill, courage, and love for children keep them in the classrooms giving their best for a stronger America . . .

To concerned parents who, like me, want the best educational experiences available for their growing children . . .

To the children in my family—Brandon, Cassidy, Cody, Cristina, Dustin, Eden, Liza, Oceana, Sol, and Wade . . . I hope my sisters, brother, and step-children will find parenting their children through public elementary school years more rewarding as a result of this book.

Contents

the educational needs of their individual communities. Encourages parents to form EPCAR (Educational Planner and Child Advocate/Representative) groups for educational excellence.

Foreword

The big day has arrived. Your child is going to enter a public school and you're desperately searching the bookshelves for guidance. Perhaps you're apprehensive because of some unfortunate childhood school experiences of your own, or because your friends with school-age children have shared a few of their school-related problems with you, or because you've been reading literature and watching television reports about the system's overwhelming problems.

Maybe you already have children enrolled in public schools and you need help in coping with difficult teachers, or perhaps you're satisfied with the teachers but have an uneasy feeling that your child may not be participating in "quality" educational programs.

It is for you and your children, and for the children in my family, that I have written this self-help book. I wanted to help parents understand how to cope creatively with difficult, contemporary public elementary school problems. This book discloses system secrets that parents need to know if they want to contribute positively to their child's academic successes. The skills provided are immediately and practically usable and can help parents help their children survive and win within the current public school structure.

When I talk with mothers and fathers about the content of this book, their consistent response is, "Where was this help when my kids were in elementary school?", or "I can't wait until publication; we have a problem now."

If you have decided to read this book, you're giving your child a rare gift, your time—time to read the book, and I hope time to apply what you'll learn. We parents spend an enormous amount of *money* on our children—their clothing, cars, vacations, cosmetic and medical attention, and education. Yet, *time* spent in our children's best interest is at least of equal value if not more. This book is dedicated to helping you gain the best the system has to offer your child. It will take some of your time, but the benefits are immeasurable.

A friend, Kim, who helped to type this book, called one evening to tell me that her daughter had come home from school crying about a problem with one of her teachers. Kim said that she used a skill and secret that she had learned from this book to deal with the situation and got wonderful results. With no conflict and without creating future difficulties, the problem was resolved to the satisfaction of all. It gives me great pleasure that before this book was even off the press it relieved a child of an unnecessary burden.

In hopes of helping many others, I humbly share with you my personal experiences and professional knowledge: knowledge that may unlock the sometimes intimidating school doors through which your child passes every day; knowledge that can help you gain some control over your child's public school destiny. If the book is helpful to even one child and family, it has been well worth the past two years to write it.

This book actually began in 1972, my first year of teaching. Since that time I have taught students from kindergarten to college in traditional and nontraditional school settings, and served public schools in several capacities. As the primary specialist for two schools, I served over 900 kindergarten through third grade students, their families and teachers. During that time I was responsible for coordinating the volunteer programs in both schools. One program exceeded sixty-five active volunteers and was recognized by the county and the state for its excellence. When I entered administration, I first served as a program coordinator for home-school education programs that aided several hundred kindergarten through fifth grade children and their families. A few years later, I became an administrative intern at the district level where I had an opportunity to facilitate the efforts of a team of outstanding professionals in the development of a comprehensive Internal Instructional District Audit. In August of 1984, I resigned from my administrative position as the assistant principal for a large elementary school. I wanted to focus my attention on the completion of this book, a writing career, and efforts to add a new member to our family.

The school district in which I was employed was and is considered by the state as one of its finest. I am proud to have been a part of its educational program. In spite of some of the unfortunate personal experiences I will share with you, most of my experiences were positive, just as most of your experiences with public schools will probably be positive ones. But, a word of caution. Parents are often led to believe that the public school system is the guardian of equal educational opportunity for all. The realities are somewhat less encouraging, realities which I feel a moral and professional obligation to share with parents. A single child's needs can be overlooked as the system struggles to care for the many.

This is a positive book, intended to answer questions that parents haven't "insider knowledge" enough to know to ask, or have asked and have received unsatisfactory replies. I'm by no means suggesting that I have all of the answers to the problems facing education in the '80s. Nor am I egocentric or foolish enough to imply that the secrets and skills shared will apply equally to every school district and every child. However, though school districts differ in the degree and kinds of problems they face and in the quality of responses to their problems, most of the secrets revealed in this book are intrinsic to public education in general, and the skills are universally applicable because they customize time-honored interpersonal techniques to the specialized relationships related to our no longer little or red schoolhouses. As a part of an ongoing concern for excellence in education, *Secrets* is, for me, the next logical step in my commitment to educational improvement for children.

Identifying the district and state where I was employed is unimportant to the essence of this book. It is sufficient to know that it is a typical, medium-to-large-sized school district with generic problems. My personal anecdotes are tools used to better illustrate the relevance of the secrets and skills that can help parents help their children happily flourish within the public school systems throughout our fifty states. To protect the identities of children, parents, teachers, and administrators, all names and grade-level references have been changed.

Throughout this book, out of respect for the comfortable and correct use of the English language and for all of my readers, the masculine and feminine pronouns have been randomly assigned. I apologize to all those "hims" and "hers" who have other style preferences, but my goal was to use the simplest and most direct means to communicate my concerns for all of our children.

TERRY FRITH

1

A Letter to Amy: Why Parents Should Become Involved in Their Child's Public School Education

My Dear Sister, Amy,

Have I told you lately how much I love your children? Cassidy is a delight—beautiful, intellectually gifted, and charming. Cody, ready to begin kindergarten, is refreshingly excited about going to school and open to new learning. Dustin, the last child, an infant I held at birth, smiling as she entered the world, holds a special place in my heart and grips my soul with the thrill of her life just beginning. Each child is uniquely precious to me. If they learn to love themselves and others, respect their abilities, appreciate their many blessings, and confidently explore life's adventures, the rewards of love and achievement will abound. As parents, you and Raymond definitely score a "10"! You take your parenting responsibilities seriously, always giving the children your best efforts, helping them grow in predictably positive directions. But, Amy, I'm concerned about their educational experiences in public schools, experiences that are profoundly important, yet unpredictable.

Cody is energy personified, curious about everything, a

happy, confident little boy. He needs a first school year with a teacher who is consistent, loving, patient, and firm; one who will appreciate his specialness and challenge his many abilities. He has "10"-quality parents. He needs "10"-quality teachers, as well.

I regret to tell you that in my experience the "10's" are outnumbered by the "1's," and the majority of teachers are between "8's" and "3's." During my eleven years as a teacher, program coordinator, primary specialist, and school administrator, I witnessed untold hours of absolutely wasted prime instructional time, physical and mental abuses inflicted by teachers, classroom environments that lacked any semblance of safety, and administrators who avoided confrontation and their responsibilities to resolve problems. Parents were not advised that their children were enduring daily indignities and suffering from lack of achievement and self-esteem as a result of incompetent teacher behavior. The system protected itself and guarded its secrets from the "outsiders," you and other parents. I was part of that system and party to protecting its inadequacies.

As a parent, you protect your children first. Everything else is secondary. For you, the system exists purely to serve children. It is your love for them and possibly some of your own unfortunate childhood school experiences that cause you to continually seek accurate information about the quality of their instructional programs and teachers. And, Amy, believe me, you need that information. While nature designed our children to blossom and grow to their full potential, as beautiful, creative, and unique in their maturity as promised in their infancy, most never achieve this ultimate fulfillment. The great minds in psychology agree on at least one thing: Fewer than 10 percent of us become mature, self-actualizing adults. To the other 90 percent, something regrettable happens between infancy and adulthood that alters their life course from one of nature's design, a life of happiness and fulfillment, to one of undesirable compromise. Childhood experiences, especially those at home and school, have a dramatic influence upon that course. Amy, you can exercise control over both of those environments and help your children become part of the fortunate 10 percent.

Traditional parent-school interaction (PTA/PTO, open house, Back to School Night, school plays, bulletins, conferences, and teacher notes) provide some of the information you seek, but you know that this communication is censored and gives you an incomplete picture of your children's school day. In your search for uncensored communication, you ask them questions as they return from school in hopes that their answers will help you responsibly monitor and support their growth and development. But can they give you unbiased, clear accounts of the day's events?

Children have limited perspectives. They have little context for their perceptions and few tools to analyze them. They do not realize that their daily experiences are forming their attitudes about themselves and their abilities; that they are storing positive or negative messages about self-esteem, self-respect, and self-acceptance; that they are constructing future goals and defining adult success and failure. They don't know that physical abuse by teachers is not an effective professional technique or that sarcasm, ridicule, and diminished self-esteem are not their just desserts for an incorrect answer. It doesn't occur to them that their achievement is poor because the teacher lacks lesson plans and organizational skills, that their ten-minutes-per-day reading instruction program is only one-twentieth of that required by the state, or that their teacher is on an annual contract as the result of a previously unacceptable job performance with other children.

Amy, you are quite right to want to know what is going on at school. Until parents recognize the value of planned, purposeful school involvement, experiences that may cause children to dread school and minimize their potential will remain in the control of the adults whom they will *randomly* encounter. Their probable academic and personal success rides on the luck of the draw. Those odds are not good enough for your children or mine. Not only do we need to *ask what happens at school,* but we need to *know how to control what happens.*

We can and should actively shape school experiences into positive, productive, successful benefits for each child. We, parents, are their childhood "Indian Guides," providers, supporters, and adoring fans. More than anyone, we love them and care about their academic, social, and emotional maturation. Who better than we should strive to prevent unnecessary problems and to represent them at school when problems do arise? Who better than we should have a comprehensive view of each child's academic program and assume an active role in monitoring and planning that program? We are potentially their best representatives, advocates, and educational planners. Yet, feelings of educational inadequacy, lack of confidence, helplessness to control the institutional complexities, or blind faith in the professional educator prevent many of us from learning how to become responsible in those roles.

Through many hours of struggle, self-discipline, and determination I've written this book as a genuine expression of love for you and your children and for parents like you who seriously want to develop competence as Educational Planners and Child Advocate/Representatives, who want firsthand uncensored school-parent communication, and who want decisive and positive answers to questions and remedies for problems. Standard system answers like "We're making efforts to improve," are pleasantries that may fill the mind tanks of future generations but, today, leave our children educationally on "empty."

So, Amy, here it is, my gift—years of enriching educational programs for your children. Mastering the skills identified in this book may be challenging, but being a parent is challenging, and you are a "10." With a little perseverance you'll be a "10" Educational Planner and Child Advocate/Representative. Even if you feel that you're less than a "10" in these new roles, not to worry. Just reading this book is an excellent first step toward upgrading your children's education. You're already a wonderful sister, woman, and mother. *Go for it!*

All my love,

Terry

CHILDREN GROW AND PARENT ROLES EXPAND—TWO NEW ROLES

Child Advocate/Representative (A/R)

Your children have a tremendous advantage: They have you! You're willing to take decisive action to see to it that they have many opportunities to enjoy life's advantages. You know that parenting is a mixed blessing: demanding and delightful; frustrating and fulfilling. You are morally committed to keeping your children physically and spiritually healthy; but can your parenting efforts stop there? Your children are presently, or soon will be, experiencing one of the greatest influences upon their lives—the public school system. While attempting to meet the needs of the many, this institutionalized system can overlook the needs of an individual child. Its inconsistent and complex nature demands that every child have adequate representation, an advocate who acts in a similar capacity to an attorney, who, unlike an attorney, receives no monetary reward, and who unselfishly devotes single-minded attention to one child. This challenging role is best filled by a loving parent, one who is concerned, genuinely supportive, and interested in becoming a child's Advocate/Representative.

Just as attorneys develop skills and expertise and use their knowledge of the law to work within the judicial system, Child Advocate/Representatives can develop skills and expertise and use their knowledge of public schools to work within the educational system. Working within this system doesn't necessarily mean accepting employment or a volunteer position within a school, becoming a room-mother/father, or seeking PTA/PTO leadership. It does suggest enlightened, ethical manipulation of a public institution for the multiple advantages it can offer your child. With working knowledge of the system's limitations and strengths you can become an effective Child Advocate/Representative.

Educational Planner (EP)

Planning a child's educational program is as critical a parenting task as planning and preparing nutritious meals. Each takes time and each is essential to a child's healthy development. In cooperation with school personnel, an Educational Planner plans and oversees his/her child's individualized instructional program. An EP learns how to confer with teachers, observe in classrooms, analyze and evaluate the use of instructional time, establish educational goals, and monitor each child's school progress.

NOTE TO AMY: Please don't be intimidated and immobilized by the apparent weight of these two new tasks, tasks that until now you may not have known existed. These roles can be as demanding and time-consuming as you choose, and as your individual child's needs dictate. Parenting has, thus far, been a difficult and rewarding journey. Probably you were a little uncertain of your abilities when you began, but your confidence grew as you became more familiar with your responsibilities and successfully coped with each new demand. You discovered that: Success + Familiarity = Confidence!

WHAT CAN EP-A/R SKILLS DO FOR
YOU AND YOUR CHILD?

Developing EP-A/R skills will help you know how to:

• Have your child assigned to the "better" teachers' classes;
• Plan a "total" individualized educational program;
• Communicate effectively during parent/administrator/teacher/team conferences;
• Analyze and improve the quality of your child's instructional schedule;
• Change your child's class assignment to an acceptable teacher when the current teacher is unacceptable;
• Use simple checklist forms to analyze teacher, curriculum, and specific program acceptability for your child;
• Become a positive Child Advocate/Representative;
• Generate positive "interpersonal interest-bearing accounts" for your child;
• Manage instructional school time—Instructional Time Management (ITM).

This book will show you how to control your personal school-related inhibitors: *fear* of conferences, *insecurity* about insufficient educational program knowledge, *confusion,* and *anger.* It can help you ethically manage the controllable aspects of the system that affect your child. Knowledge + Skill = Control. Your confidence will abound, stimulated by newly acquired knowledge, EP-A/R skills, and familiarity with the system.

THE INVISIBLE SYSTEM

Functioning in every school district are two distinct educational systems: one, formal and clearly visible; the other,

informal and camouflaged. The formal structure has an organizational flow chart that outlines the chain of command. Job
descriptions exist for each position on that chart. (For an example, see chart on page 26.) Learning about your district's
formal system, its policies, procedures, and guidelines, requires minimal research and effort. Simply go to any district
level office or school and ask to see the County/District Policy and Procedures Manuals. They are usually voluminous
and are best used as references. While knowledge of the visible system is beneficial, this book is about the unwritten, informal system, an invisible structure that creates its own
interpersonal and intrapersonnel rules, policies, guidelines,
and procedures—all networked with "secrets" commonly
shared within the profession and routinely guarded from the
public the system serves. These secrets are not devious plots
at work in public education to deceive or abuse you or your
children. They are a characteristic outgrowth of the institution's attempt to protect itself against its employees and
against the general public. Because parents, teachers, and
teachers' unions attack the institution with lawsuits and grievances when they believe their rights have been abused, the
system understandably remains closed about moral, legal, and
political issues that could make it vulnerable to these attacks.
For example: *Parade* magazine, January 15, 1984, stated:

> A 65 page report issued by the National Commission on
> Excellence in Education, titled *A Nation at Risk,* scathingly
> declares that "the educational foundations of our society
> are presently being eroded by a rising tide of mediocrity
> that threatens our very future as a nation and a people." . . .
> Another organization, the National Science Teachers' Asso-
> ciation, reports that almost 40% of the country's math and
> science teachers are probably unqualified to teach those
> subjects.

The fact that there are many unqualified teachers is certainly no secret. Competence—one of the most explosive,

conflict-producing school issues—is safely discussed as an impersonal statistic. If, however, the system specifically identified the names of the individuals at your child's school who were among the 40 percent of unqualified math and science teachers, then the institution would suffer legal and political reprisal. The teachers involved would file suit; the unions would attack; and now officially informed, you could sue the system claiming that your child's rights had been knowingly abused. Furthermore, professional ethics prohibit a principal from informing you that your child is assigned to a marginally competent or an incompetent teacher. End result, the teacher's rights are protected and your child bears the consequences.

Now a few secrets are born. While faculty at your child's school know of those teachers who are outstandingly skilled and those who are marginally acceptable, you cannot be permitted to know those secrets or the secrets that would help you have your child assigned to the "better" teachers. The teacher competency tragedy is only one of the multicomplex problems waging war on our public schools and creating professional secrets within the structured invisible system.

The secrets I share in this book can help you help your children survive and win within public schools. Used prudently and wisely, your awareness of these secrets will:

- Provide information from "within" the invisible system;
- Give you uncensored decision-making data for effective educational planning;
- Motivate you to learn Child Advocate/Representative (A/R) skills to cope creatively with school personnel;
- Enlighten you about the controllable aspects of public schools;
- Help you provide the best possible public school education available for your child.

A TYPICAL ORGANIZATIONAL CHART

SCHOOL BOARD OF ANONYMOUS DISTRICT

SUPERINTENDENT OF SCHOOLS

ASSISTANT SUPERINTENDENT FOR INSTRUCTION

ASSISTANT SUPERINTENDENT FOR NONINSTRUCTIONAL SERVICES

DIRECTOR Curr. & Staff Dev.
- SUPERVISOR Reading
- SUPERVISOR Science
- SUPERVISOR Language Arts
- SUPERVISOR Social Studies
- SUPERVISOR Mathematics
- SUPERVISOR Music
- SUPERVISOR Phys. Ed.
- SUPERVISOR Ed. Media
- SUPERVISOR Health Ed. & Services
- COORDINATOR Measurement & Research
- COORDINATOR Volunteer Serv. & Public Info.
- SUPERVISOR Art

DIRECTOR Secondary Ed.
- Principals Middle & High Schools

DIRECTOR Elementary Ed.
- Principals Elementary
- COORDINATOR Student Accounting

DIRECTOR Student Services & Excep. Stud. Ed.
- School Psychologist
- School Social Worker I & II
- Placement & Follow-Up Spec.
- COORDINATORS Excep. Stud. Ed.
- COORDINATOR Guid. Couns.

DIRECTOR Vocational Tech. & Adult Ed.
- DIRECTOR Voc. & Tech. Center
- SUPERVISOR Voc. Home Ec.
- COORDINATOR Adult Ed. & SUPERVISOR Business Education
- SUPERVISOR Voc. Agriculture & Ind. Arts

DIRECTOR Personnel Relations

DIRECTOR Personnel Services

DIRECTOR Planning, Reports, Fed. Prog.
- COORDINATOR E.C.I.A.
- COORDINATOR Child Migrant

DIRECTOR Food Service
- Assistant Director Food Service
- Cafeteria Managers

DIRECTOR Operations, Maint. & Trans.
- SUPERVISOR Operations & Energy
- SUPERVISOR Buildings & Grounds
- SUPERVISOR Veh. & Equip. Maint.
- SUPERVISOR School Bus Operations

DIRECTOR Budget & Finance
- Manager Payroll
- Manager Spec. Rev. Accting.
- SUPERVISOR Accounting

DIRECTOR Materials & Serv.
- Buyers
- Manager Stores

Manager Projects
- DIRECTOR Data Processing

BEGIN NOW, NOW, NOW, NOW, NOW

There are many serious issues facing public schools and parents. However, while we try to work together toward the betterment of all, your child could be wasting prime educational years in his/her life today. This book will focus on the present because your child is growing up now! Your actions and attitudes could help or hinder your child's educational future. It's true that your parental actions should have nothing to do with your child's public education program. By law, all children should receive an equal education. It would, however, be naive of you to believe that this actually is the case. Focus on the facts, secrets, and skills in this book. Learn to have a positive affect upon your child's educational destiny. Precious time could be lost if we devote too much attention to "Ain't the school system awful," "How it should be," and "But the law says." These concerns for the future of education which are discussed in the last chapter are legitimate and deserve your attention, but not to the exclusion of your child's present educational needs.

There are many talented, dedicated teachers and school administrators who do provide competent, constructive, and child-centered educational programs. These are the individuals you want to teach your children. However, it has been my professional and personal experience that in many schools there are only a few excellent teachers, several totally unacceptable teachers, and the majority variously skilled instructors ranking somewhere between the two polarities, excellent and poor.

Suppose that two incapable teachers teach 25 children per year. Then 50 children a year in one school lose valuable educational time. (In some team teaching situations and open space instruction many more children are affected, but for now let's assume we're considering a self-contained traditional classroom structure.) If there are 30 elementary schools in one district multiplied by the 50 students per school, then 1500 students did not receive even an adequate education for that year. Multiply 1500 students by the number of districts in a state. Florida has 67 districts; 67 districts times 1500 students equals 100,500 students per year in one state who are seriously deprived of an education. Imagine the gravity of the problem if those teachers are permitted to teach for 30 years to retirement. Carry this conjecture to its logical conclusion. Multiply the 100,500 students in one state by our 50 states and 5,025,000 students per year in the U.S. are innocent victims of educational deprivation. Remember that the 5,025,000 figure is based upon an assumption that every public elementary school has two inadequate teachers with approximately 25 students, and that each state had 67 districts and 30 elementary schools per district. This probably is a gross miscalculation. I was employed in several elementary schools that had at least three individuals whom I would have evaluated as totally unacceptable to teach children. This is not an attempt to sensationalize. It is a genuine effort to encourage parents and educators to analyze the reality of permitting incompetence in our classrooms.

TRAINING BEGINS WITH INSIGHT

Let's begin our Educational Planner and Child Advocate/Representative training program by appreciating what can happen to children in the normal course of a day in public school. I have two main objectives for sharing these experiences. One, it's critical to *enlighten parents* and concerned others about the injustice, abuse, inhumanity, and instructional deprivation that are currently occurring every day in our public schools. Two, it's essential to *encourage all parents to recognize the need for immediate action* to protect their children today as well as working together in our communities for a stronger educational tomorrow.

The following events, which I personally witnessed, occurred in several elementary schools within the past few years:

• On a very hot day, an elementary school teacher made his entire class stand on one leg on a blacktop pavement on the playground for a full thirty minutes. One child fainted. This treatment was administered to the class as punishment for talking without permission. Two other teachers observed this tactic and adopted it for future class punishment.

• A teacher observed two of her fifth grade students "humping" the wall in the boys' bathroom. As punishment she made them "hump" a wall in front of the entire class. The class was told to watch while the boys were ridiculed.

• A first grade teacher told a child to stand in the trash can because "He behaved like trash and therefore belonged with trash."

• A second grade teacher often knocked children's heads together, pulled their ears, pinched their noses, and isolated them in closets. This was always accompanied by daily yelling and verbal abuses.

• A master teacher kept an annual behavior chart which indicated with check marks the names of children who misbehaved. With three checks by a child's name, a spanking was administered. Often, ten children per day were paddled by the administration at the teacher's request. Occasionally, when an administrator wasn't available, the teacher spanked the children.

• On a day when the temperature was well into the 90s, a fifth grade teacher turned off all the fans in an unairconditioned classroom, made all of the children get down on their knees at their desks, closed the doors and windows, and would not permit anyone to get water or to use the bathroom facilities until assignments were completed. He daily ridiculed, belittled, and verbally tormented children. These gestapo techniques were standard procedure for this teacher.

• Each day after lunch one assistant teacher was assigned to supervise approximately 150 first grade students for a period of thirty minutes to an hour. Even a highly skilled teacher could not responsibly supervise such a large group for this period of time. Not only was the safety of children jeopardized, but the school administration made itself foolishly vulnerable.

• A third grade teacher's students were permitted to crawl on the floor, stand on desks, fight, stand on chairs, and in general behave in ways which were detrimental to a stable learning environment and to the children's safety. This behavior occurred every day, all day. If any instruction was provided, it was incidental and unplanned. No planned instruction was apparent.

• A teacher had a row of children called the "dummy row." She made this known to students and faculty. On one occasion she hit a child in the face with a book. Once when the school facility was under construction and a particular section was roped off for the protection of students and teachers, and clearly marked "Danger, Do not walk here," this teacher took the entire class under the rope and through the "Danger Zone."

• A teacher would often tie a child in his chair. She explained that he needed a lot of water and it was disruptive for him to get up so often. I inquired about the parents' feelings regarding roping him in his chair. She informed me that his parents were uneducated and probably did things at home to him that were much worse than anything she could do.

• After her students colored pictures/assignments, this same teacher would have them come to the front of the room to display their work for everyone. Then she would make remarks about every drawing such as, "You didn't stay in the lines," "You have too much blue in yours," etc. Several children were reduced to tears during these episodes. What could possibly have been her educational objective?

• A young teacher in the same school as the teacher in the example above tried to encourage me to use a "rope" to tie disruptive children in their chairs. She claimed it was a very effective technique she had learned from that teacher.

• A fourth grade child who played with a pencil and disrupted class was disciplined by being forced to get down on his hands and knees, place his hands behind his back, and roll the pencil with his nose. He was told to do this the entire length of a fifty-foot corridor, back and forth, several times while the whole class watched and laughed.

• Because a third grade child was disruptive in class, he was tested and considered for the EH (Emotionally Handicapped) Program. After appropriate administrative intervention the child was tested and eventually placed in the Gifted Program. His unacceptable classroom behavior completely disappeared. Two years later, he is progressing well. His progress report would be entirely different if he had been misplaced in the EH Program when he was obviously gifted and not emotionally disturbed.

• A second grade child, whose medical record indicated a kidney problem, wet her pants in class because the teacher refused to let her go to the bathroom during instruction.

• A teacher in an open concept, "differentiated staffing" school spent most of the day, every day, in the teachers' office work area and assigned her aide to teach the class. The aide had a high school diploma. (It is common practice in differentiated staffing to officially assign students to assistant teachers who may have only a two-year degree. This supposedly is to be completely under the direction of the "master" teacher, who also has a full class and the additional responsibility of supervising the planning for and instruction of the assistant teacher's classes. In effect, the students received instruction from two-year-degree personnel, and the district hired the assistants for almost half the price of certificated teachers.)

These fifteen stories highlight just a few incidents. *The following is an overview of incidents that occurred several times and were too numerous to give individual attention.*

• Children went without the appropriate program evaluation, staffing, and placement, because teachers didn't want to do the necessary paperwork required for initial referral to Special Student Services/Exceptional Child Education Programs.

• Instructional lesson plans were not written for weeks at a time. No goals, no objectives, no daily, weekly, monthly, quarterly, semester, or annual plans of any kind were apparent during instruction. Endless handouts of mimeographed paperwork for "busy" assignments replaced the planned, purposeful instruction that children should have rightfully received.

• Children were subjected to intimidation, threats, screaming, belittling, and ridicule.

• Teachers physically abused children—pinching, pushing, hitting, pulling ears and hair.

• Hours upon hours of instructional time were wasted with films, movies, records, and slides that were used as time fillers rather than appropriate instructional tools clearly designed to compliment specific objectives.

- Entire planning days were wasted as a few teachers chatted for hours or played games such as chess and gin rummy.

- Teacher unions sought or created issues to defend in order to justify their existence. School Board hearings regarding teacher grievances often take hours of the Board's time as well as that of instructional and administrative personnel. This is costly to the taxpayer.

- Children lost valuable instructional hours because classroom teachers, special program teachers, and federal program teachers could not effectively schedule time and plan an integrated curriculum for each child. (Further explained in Chapter 6.)

- Assistant teachers taught children all year as their primary instructor.

- There were guidance programs in which guidance counselors were unable to devote time to their priority tasks of counseling students because they were assigned so many quasi-administrative or clerical tasks.

These alarming and frightening stories have been shared to alert you to the fact that your child may very well be in a totally unacceptable school environment. So you ask, "Why wouldn't my children tell me?" Sometimes they do. It's important to listen to what your child tells you and then to ask pertinent questions which will lead to more specific information. Often children are too young and inarticulate to explain events in adult language. However, many children believe they deserve the teachers' mistreatment. They are often reluctant to tell parents because they fear further consequences. And of course, they are not mature enough to analyze the quality of an instructional program. For example, they might think that a movie/cartoon was great fun. The film would not have to have an instructional objective for them to enjoy it.

There are professionally acceptable maneuvers which ultimately afford some children better educational environments than others. One of the most critical administrative maneuvers is assigning competent teachers to instruct children with specific problems.

Permit me to explain. Obviously, all children attending public elementary school are assigned to a teacher or teachers. The question becomes, which child to which teacher(s). The maneuvers occur when initially assigning students. For example, children who suffer from a serious illness such as diabetes, epilepsy, or leukemia need to be assigned to extremely alert decision-makers who know when and how to take appropriate action in the event of an emergency. These children shouldn't be assigned to teachers who would walk children through a zone roped off and marked "Danger, Do Not Enter," as the teacher did in the vignette on p. 30. It is essential that those who are responsible for the health and safety of these "high health risk children" possess the highest degree of professional expertise as well as good common sense. While it is administratively irresponsible to assign any child to an incompetent teacher, it is criminal to assign an unhealthy child to an adult who could in fact endanger that child's life.

Then, of course, the children who are in special student service programs, those who have severe specific learning disabilities, social/emotional problems, those who are gifted and need to be challenged and accepted, the withdrawn, the overly aggressive, and those who do not qualify for any special student service program but require extraordinary additional attention must be considered for classroom assignments to reliable, competent, capable professionals.

The teacher(s) assignment will predictably afford some children better educational opportunities than other children. Perhaps now you can better appreciate some of the critical decisions involved when assigning children to teachers. The students' physical health and safety are the first priority, usually followed by a consideration of emotional disorders and educational problems, and concerns for educational excellence are relegated to last place.

Now the question comes home to rest with you, "What teacher(s) will be assigned to my child?" While the school and district curriculum and philosophy are important ingredients for a comprehensive, respectable educational program, the teachers are the vehicles that communicate, interpret, and convey the curriculum to the students.

It's up to you to have the very best instruction for your child. Surprise! You didn't know it was in your control. You didn't know that your children can have the better instructors. But do you know how to recognize the most qualified, excellent teachers? What criteria are used to determine teacher excellence? Do you have the time and expertise to determine teacher acceptability for your child?

In the following chapters, we will explore some answers to those questions, identify EP-A/R goals and skills, and reveal school system secrets.

2
Initial School Enrollment: The Critical Beginning

Those most skilled in human relations recognize the value of planning productive, constructive communication. Prior to any interaction with school personnel, an EP-A/R would be wise to prepare for and plan the development of relationships. It's possible that considering premeditated, purposeful approaches to human encounters may give you the uneasy feeling of being manipulative. If so, consider that although manipulation may be in some instances an abuse of human dignity, it also is at the heart of many thoughtful and meaningful exchanges. Once you are aware of the value of a smile or a kind word, then to use them *is* to manipulate even when your goal is to enrich a moment of another's time. Manipulation is not always ugly; sometimes it represents the very essence of caring. If your intentions are to ensure the educational, social, and emotional welfare of your children, then, surely there is nothing underhanded or sneaky in ethically using knowledge and skills to achieve this purpose. You will not be furthering your own interests at anyone's expense. It is moral and responsible to protect your child and to work toward the mutual cooperation and interests of the educational system and your family.

Enrolling a child in a new elementary school or in school for the first time ever can be a confusing experience for parents. Yet the original contact with the school will begin a relationship which often determines the selection of your child's teachers for as long as he/she remains in that school. At this particular time it is critical to have skills which will allow you to transcend the confusion and to control in a constructive manner the outcome of the enrollment process.

Teaching, just as any profession, has those in its ranks who excel and those who are "hangers-on." The eagles soar and work hard, and the buzzards scavenge the leftovers, giving little in return for their meals. You want eagles for your child, not buzzards.

It is common practice that parents are not permitted to select classroom teachers for their child. Occasionally a written statement to that affect is specified in a school/district policy manual. Ironically, parents select their child's physician, minister, and extracurricular teachers (for instance, piano and ballet), but they are discouraged from making any input in selecting those who, next to themselves, will probably have the most formative role in the lives of their children during their elementary school years. Some of the fortunate are assigned to eagles. The public school system has multicomplex reasons for strategically discouraging the general public's selection of classroom teachers. Remember that our objective is not at present to change the system, but to cope with it. Therefore, I will not address the system's rationale for restricting parents from active teacher selection. In many instances because of our mobile society, even if parents were given a choice of teachers, they wouldn't know whom to select. Learning EP-A/R interpersonal skills will allow you to appropriately intercede during the enrollment process and secure an excellent or acceptable teacher even when you don't know any of the teachers' professional reputations.

ENROLLMENT GOALS: TO SECURE AN EAGLE FOR YOUR CHILD.

TO BUILD THE BASIS FOR A POSITIVE, CONSTRUCTIVE SCHOOL RELATIONSHIP.

▷ **Secret # 1:**

During the enrollment process you may be told something such as, "All student names are fed into the computer and it places students," or "It is policy that parents are not permitted to select a teacher." Do not be discouraged by these comments. Multitudes of children enroll and withdraw every year. School personnel who deal with these issues genuinely and justifiably tire of the traffic. Policies are often impatiently quoted as a routine response to insistent parents. Surely Confucious must have said that "the more stable the student population, the less weary and more patient the school staff."

Be calm, poised, and friendly. Accept their policy and procedure comments with grace, assured in the knowledge that **you can exert some control over the teacher selection process, particularly during the initial enrollment procedure.**

Computers do not place children in classrooms. People who feed information into computers make the decisions. Contrary to popular belief, that convenient, mysterious computer can be controlled.

▷ **Secret # 2: The school administration, faculty, and office staff know who are the most dedicated, talented educators within their facility.**

As professionals, they work intimately with one another. They problem-solve, conduct staff development programs, seek advice and support from colleagues, visit the teachers' lounge for breaks, train and utilize volunteer services, attend conferences, and meetings, plan curricula, order materials, and participate together in various other activities.

Eagles are characteristically appreciated by parents, students, and faculty. Their skillful, planned, stimulating instruction earns the respect and love of the students. Their genuinely expressed regard for children, their rights, their academic, social, and emotional progress bridges the parent-professional communication gap. Colleagues who are not poisoned with professional jealousy respect the eagles' ability, seek their counsel and friendship, admire their leadership and quality of character. Even the buzzards recognize eagles. Occasionally a hostile-aggressive buzzard attempts to clip the wings of an eagle. This is unwise of the buzzard and seems to occur infrequently because eagles usually have the support of the school staff.

Paradoxically, it is considered "generally unprofessional" to openly acknowledge and emphasize differences between eagles and buzzards. A secretary or school administrator would cause serious morale problems, be criticized by the professional staff, and be vulnerable to grievances and suits if he editorialized to parents about the strengths and weaknesses of teachers. For example: "Mrs. J. is our most sensitive, creatively skilled instructor in third grade. Unfortunately, there is no more room in her class. Your child must be assigned to Mrs. S., who lacks patience with students, hates teaching, is looking for another job, and sits disinterestedly behind her desk most of the day."

Perhaps you're thinking, "Why doesn't the administrator work toward dismissal of these incompetents?" Myron Lieberman, president of Educational Services in Modesto, California, stated in a *Phi Delta Kappan* article about teacher bargaining, that, ". . . a teachers' union tends to negotiate protective measures sought by its constituents. Thus the slob wants the union's protection against dress codes. . . . The marginal teacher wants to restrict observations and evaluations, so as to weaken or cripple administrative efforts to terminate teachers. And so the teacher union tries to negotiate such protections—and it often succeeds."

Unions and potential "competence" litigation in my estimation are the primary reasons that buzzards are in the system now and will be in the foreseeable future. Although teacher pay scales provide for difference in education and seniority, they rarely acknowledge the real differences in ability which range from outstanding to grossly unacceptable.

Florida's recent short-sighted, poorly instituted, but well-intended attempt to acknowledge differences in ability by providing a merit pay program is probably foredoomed largely because of the teachers' union. The union has devised roadblocks which could render the entire merit pay system useless. It continues to insist that it is impossible to fairly and prescriptively pay instructors according to the quality of job performance. Thus, mediocrity is protected and encouraged. If fair evaluation is impossible, then there can be no legally defensible definition of "incompetence." For example, in Polk County, Florida, 1984, the school system may have to forfeit $700,000 of state funding because the union persuaded teachers to undermine the use of the state-adopted merit pay program.

In September 1984, on nationwide television, a three-hour ABC special highlighting problems in our public schools entitled, "To Save Our Schools: To Save Our Children," stated, "The unions . . . have protected their weakest members rather than winning rewards for their strongest. . . . The result is that the quality of teaching suffers. . . . NEA and local chapters resist merit pay programs and teacher competency tests."

Their insistence that all should receive equal pay according to clearly defined pay scales ignoring differences in quality of performance is a commentary on either their lack of ingenuity or integrity. Some teachers positively accept this position of equal pay for all regardless of performance because of the pressure of union politics. Others aggressively supply fuel to the flame because their very souls are permeated with the fear of being singled out and publicly recognized as buzzards. Others who believe in merit pay fight an uphill battle against union politics, institutional ineptitude, and social passivity as they strive to institute financial rewards for superior performance.

Though unions have been in the past and still could be credible professional organizations which resolve conflicts, seek improved educational environments and programs, and champion substantial causes promoting improved teacher performance, they too often have become demotivating forces which seek to prove their usefulness by inventing causes to defend. Their express purposes for existence are often worthy and needed. In practice, unfortunately, they frequently distort truth for self-serving motives, negotiate for the incompetent, and plan periodic distress and political tension. "To Save Our Schools: To Save Our Children" also reported that in the last forty-three years only eighty-six tenured teachers have been dismissed for incompetence in the entire nation.

Despite these protestations of "no differences among the troops," there is a token acknowledgment for exceptional job performance entitled "Teacher of the Year." This title highlights an individual in each district, then each state, and ultimately one is recognized as "Teacher of the Year" for the United States. I've often wondered why one individual is selected as "Teacher of the Year." We should have so many eagles that it would be practically impossible to select the annual eagle of eagles.

When you enroll your child, if you make a remark such as, "I want a very good teacher who will have a lot of patience with my child," you're likely to get the stock response, "All of our teachers are certificated by the State and qualified to teach." That request will not predictably produce the results you seek. The administrator is obliged to represent her faculty as equally qualified. Furthermore, ironically, a direct "I want the best," may be interpreted as pushy, aggressive, or naive rather than a genuine concern about the classroom instructional program.

▷ **Secret # 3: Your children can be subtly punished if you (or they) disturb the school personnel's "weather conditions."**

It is human nature to desire a comfortable daily work experience. Teachers, administrators, and secretaries are no exception. No conflict, no discipline problems, no complaining parents, no accidents, no ill students, no demanding administrators, no clerical static, no fury, fuss, or flames would be an ideal daily weather forecast for working conditions. This fantasy is born of frustration and underlies basic human needs for comfort and safety. If you ruffle feathers or take an unduly critical stance, you may unwittingly influence school personnel against your child.

Moreover, intentionally or subconsciously, some teachers and perhaps an occasional administrator mistreat children for whom they harbor negative feelings. This punitive treatment may manifest itself in a variety of ways that neither administrators nor parents can monitor, such as ignoring a child's questions, avoiding responding to physical and/or emotional needs, encouraging negative self-perception, minimizing successes, abusing creative abilities, bruising egos, tormenting with nonconstructive criticism, and expressing impatience and eager disapproval. Incidentally, these teacher behaviors are extremely difficult to document. Those administrators and parents who have tried often have appeared ridiculous. For the most part A/Rs must use well-developed interpersonal skills, not muscle, in performing their tasks.

Disturbing the desired "weather conditions" in any way realistically demands that an EP-A/R carefully assess the issues, the people involved, and the consequences to his/her child as a result of positive intervention.

When possible, discuss any planned course of action with a

friend. Then practice and prepare for your successful representation.

SKILLS FOR SUCCESSFUL ENROLLMENT

▶ **Skill #1: Make a pre-enrollment appointment with the school's administrator several days before you plan to officially enroll your child.**

Let's assume that there are two administrators and two office assistants to manage a facility with 1,000 students and approximately 75 instructional and noninstructional employees. More than a hundred students enroll and withdraw during a single semester of the school year. The actual 1,000 student count remains fairly constant, but the individual students will change. They will have new faces, new names, and new but familiar problems.

With little forethought, preventative problem-solving, or strategic planning, many parents enroll their children a few days before school opens or on the first day. Their children become part of a crowd and when they are enrolled, they will get the randomly impersonal treatment of "next in line" and possibly "buzzard time."

You would be recognized as an exceptional parent to call several days in advance of enrollment, before any problems or crises have arisen, to discuss school enrollment procedures, the school's curricula, and your child's special interests and needs. You and your child have now been set apart from the 1,000 and the constant traffic. Calling for an appointment prior to initial enrollment begins the reservoir of positively expressed feelings and expectations for meaningful communication.

▶ **Skill #2:**
When you call for the appointment, begin to **build a positive relationship with the school secretary(ies).** The impression you make is important. It is an unfortunate practice, but

not unheard of, that in some schools secretaries assign children to their teachers. Whether or not this is the case in your child's school, secretaries are a vital part of the system and consciously or unconsciously have some control over daily events affecting your child. Strive to have a friendly, but brief, chat. Finally, explain that your child is going to be a new student at the school and that you would like to make an appointment with the principal to discuss your child's educational program. Remember, this first contact is crucial. Try to be as flexible, cheerful, and positive as possible. You may be referred to an assistant administrator. It's probably wise to accept the alternative offer. *The secretary may be guiding you toward the individual who will be of the most immediate help.*

Direct your thinking in this way. Ask yourself, "After a series of unpleasant encounters with an individual, do I choose his company? Do I spend my valuable time creatively assessing numerous ways in which I could assist him with problems?" Realistically, your answer to these questions is no.

As an A/R, you want and need allies. Plan to earn them. Initiating conversation which shows interest in the office staff is a simple gesture of respect and regard which usually is reciprocated in kind. Cort R. Flint, a former college president, currently a minister and contemporary author of several books including *Purpose of Love*, said, "One of the most difficult things to give away is kindness—it is usually returned."

Building a positive relationship with the office staff will prove worthwhile in future dealings with the school for appointments, records, problems, clinic assistance, classroom placement, early dismissal/withdrawal, relationships with administrators and teachers. While the office staff may have little authority in the visible structure, for better or worse, they may have immense influence within the invisible one.

SKILLS FOR POSITIVE ENCOUNTERS

Keep foremost in your thoughts that in your first encounters with the school you should be concerned with coping with the existing system, not with changing its procedures, values, or programs (see Skill # 10). Your ever-present goal is to represent your child to the best of your ability. There are several obvious, but essential, ingredients for a successful first encounter/appointment with the school administrator which are worthy of acknowledgment as skills. They can dissolve physical and social barriers, enhance nonverbal and verbal communication, and help you create a positive first impression. These same skills practiced in your subsequent dealings with the school can form the basis of a constructive working relationship with all school personnel involved with your child.

▶ **Skill # 3: Dress in a businesslike manner.**
Numerous studies emphasize that people demonstrate an elevated level of acceptance and respect for those who dress appropriately and advantageously. Obviously, one would not wear a swimsuit to church.

In his book *Communicating in Conferences*, written primarily for teachers and future teachers, Paul G. Friedman states, ". . . people feel best when interacting with others who seem similar to themselves. . . . People also tend to have greater regard for others who appear more physically attractive, better-dressed, outgoing and sociable."

You want the administrator to find commonalities as soon as she meets you. Dress is a simple first step toward mutual appreciation. It is judicious and prudent to avoid the possibility of being discounted because of inappropriate dress or grooming. Dressing as a professional administrator dresses is a concrete, nonverbal compliment to the administrator.

▶ **Skill #4: Demonstrate a sincere interest in the school's concerns.**

Asking relevant questions and listening attentively to the responses are the best expressions of genuine interest. For example, you might ask:

1. How many students are enrolled?
2. How many buses service the school, delivering and picking up students?
3. How large is the faculty?
4. Do the school test scores compare favorably with State and County scores on similar tests?

Take care that these questions are asked sympathetically and not in a grilling manner. Remember, you are visiting, not investigating. Be an interested guest, not an inquisitive detective.

▶ **Skill #5: Communicate an appreciation for school and administrative issues and your ability to assimilate new data by offering supportive comments and succinctly paraphrasing the new information.**

For example, in response to some new information a parent might comment, "With ten buses delivering students from so many areas, you not only have a large but a diverse student population. You must be very busy just with crises. It's wonderful that you find time for preventative conferences like ours."

Because it is not common practice for a parent to make an appointment prior to enrollment, the administrator might have viewed your request as a potentially unpleasant encounter. Your sincere, static-free comments will help to alleviate possible anxiety that he might feel about the purpose of the appointment.

▶ **Skill #6: Make brief and positive comments about your child.**

For example: "My child is intelligent, curious, and gets

along well with others." "Sara is so affectionate and loves to learn."

Beginning with your first encounter with school personnel and permeating all subsequent contacts, your foremost goal is to create and maintain a psychologically positive image of your child. When her name comes up at school, you want good thoughts and feelings associated with it. We all have our share of faults, children included. We have strengths and virtues as well. But school personnel often are forced to deal with crises, and they can too easily begin identifying children with their academic and social difficulties. Your child could become synonymous with the problems he creates.

Skillful Child Advocate/Representatives learn to approach school/child difficulties productively, boosting their child's image and dissipating negative, fault-finding, blaming attitudes toward her.

Certainly, children will exhibit unacceptable behavior, as we all are occasionally inclined to do. Perhaps we exceed the speed limit, stuff ourselves gluttonously at a party, or mistreat a dear friend. We experience the consequences of our behavior: a speeding violation, indigestion, or the loss of a friendship. The consequences cause us to identify and modify our behaviors—that is, they cause us to grow.

Children respond similarly. Consequences for action should teach children appropriate and constructive behavior. A verbal barrage of child-labeling, ridicule, and guilt-dumping are unacceptable responses parents often make when informed of their child's misbehavior. Furthermore, if school personnel hear you validate their negative child-image, it is not only likely that they will contact you frequently about your child's disruptive behavior, but more importantly, they will consciously or subconsciously look for justification of these mutually shared perceptions. Agreeing with any generalized, negative perception of your child only intensifies problems and becomes a psychological barrier to productive problem-solving.

I have heard countless parents who, a bit flattered to be on first name basis with their child's teacher, find it conversationally chummy to venture something like, "Mary, you must be a saint to put up with Billy. I can't imagine being with him all day. Weekends are all I can stand. Summer vacations almost do me in." The Child Advocate/Representative absolutely never does this!

I'm not suggesting that parents offer rationalizations or excuses for their child's unacceptable behavior. Excuses are detrimental to the child and to meaningful communication. For example, if a seven-year-old child steals crayons from another child, how should the responsible EP-A/R respond? Certainly you would not want school personnel to call your child a thief, nor should you categorically deny that your child could have done such a thing. The best way to handle this or similar situations is to discuss with school personnel specific objective details of the incident. The behavior is undesirable but should not develop into a full-fledged "thief for life" profile. Blame for yourself, your child, or the school has no place in this conversation. The fact remains that your child took something which didn't belong to him. The parent(s) and the school will work out mutually agreed-upon consequences. The consequences should fit the infraction and have therapeutic value. One month without a bicycle is an unreasonable and inappropriate punishment for a seven-year-old for this particular behavior. The punishment would be more closely related to the infraction if the child had to save his own money, purchase a new box of crayons, write a note of apology, and return these personally to the injured party. This example demonstrates how you, as an EP-A/R, can guide school personnel to view behavior as childlike, unacceptable, correctable, and temporary, and provide an opportunity for your child to learn and grow toward self-actualized maturity.

Practice comfortably and casually commenting about your child's specialness. Parents can become boring when they press continuously on about the marvels of their child's accomplishments. Boasting of these is not as likely to promote positive child perceptions as will occasional assertions about his/her quality of character, personality, and home/family values. Practicing with an honest, open friend will help you become more comfortable as you strive to refine this communication skill.

REMEMBER: You do not deny your child's misbehaviors. You simply do not buy into labeling his/her character as a result of them. The problems children create, if handled positively, lead to growth.

Be encouraged, because eagles are seldom frustrated with parents who express genuine respect and love for their children.

▶ **Skill #7: Make a creative "I care about education" kit,** loaded with heart-felt, responsible substance about home/ school communication. Develop a repertoire of positive ideas about public education, parent-school interaction, and the like. For example: "I have faith that the home and school can cooperatively resolve problems." "I truly care about the quality of education." Pull these goodies from your "kit" during your initial interview with the administrator and in any subsequent contact with school personnel. If your style of delivery does not resemble Pollyanna's but believably reaffirms mutual values, then school personnel will respond favorably. The goodwill you perpetuate will be well worth the effort expended in developing your kit.

▶ **Skill #8: Give notice that you will be on the scene.** During your first conference with the administration, subtly state that you will occasionally visit your child's classroom and that you'll try to help the school and teachers as much as your busy schedule will allow. Because your child has not as yet been assigned a teacher, this gives the administrator an ample, conscience-free, honorable opportunity to effortlessly assign your child to a teacher who he knows will soar like an eagle whenever you visit. Practically speaking, your dissatisfaction could lead to frequent conferences which take administrative time that is already pressed to its occasionally unmanageable limits. An astute administrator's awareness of your future classroom visits and of your obvious A/R skill would enhance the likelihood of a more than acceptable initial teacher assignment.

Parents will not regret the productive time given to their child's school. Visibility leads to personal contact. Even limited visibility that encourages goodwill will effectively produce results. Your child will reap the benefits a thousandfold in ways you may never know because of the subtle means in which the staff relates to him/her. These long-term "interest-bearing" relationships will be a direct reflection of your representation.

▶ **Skill #9: Notify appropriate school personnel orally and in writing of all health concerns and/or other critical or potential problems.**

In Chapter 1, I discussed the vital importance of assigning children with specific health concerns to teachers with demonstrated common sense and professional expertise. It would be advisable for parents to briefly but thoroughly inform the administration of all special needs your child may have. Not only will this action maximize the safety and well-being of your child, but ironically it will enhance his/her chances of being assigned to an eagle.

Also request an appointment with other appropriate personnel who will be involved as a result of your particular concerns. For example, the guidance counselor may plan programs for children who are unusually socially withdrawn. A primary specialist or curriculum specialist may be needed to assist with an individualized educational program due to your child's academic excellence (which may be neglected otherwise) or academic deficiencies. The physical education teacher may need to know about your child's health problems and the physician's recommendations for outdoor activity. Actively involve all appropriate personnel in the unusual needs of your child.

▶ **Skill # 10: Cultivate an "ally relationship" with the school personnel involved with your child.**

Use Form G, "The People at School are Special to Our Family" (explained in Chapter 8, p. 207), as a means of enhancing your relationship with school personnel. The cardinal rule for using this form is to emphasize to the school administration the form's primary purpose: to provide your family with information about the special personal and school occasions, such as birthdays, of those who work with your child. Explain that you appreciate assistance in acquiring this information because you try to teach your child that genuine expressions of respect and thoughtfulness are an important part of growing up. Interestingly enough, the administrator may be in temporary shock that a parent wants to recognize the birthdays and other special events affecting all of the professionals working with a child. This initial response should not discourage you. Accept that you've probably left an indelible card in her memory bank. Your request is unusual and administrative ambivalence is to be expected.

Reasonable initial tactics such as recognizing staff birthdays, marriages, deaths in families, honors, and new births, which identify you as a sincerely supportive parent, will begin defining you as an ally and one who will be remembered. Recognize teacher work days and national and religious holidays with cards, letters of appreciation, small gifts, and/or food.

For instance, on a work day, a single cake often provides welcome refreshment for the office staff and a grade level of teachers. They tend to remember these tangible expressions of appreciation and support. Some parents prepare vegetable trays with dip for those more health conscious. If you don't have time to prepare refreshments, a plant or a small item for the desk is always received positively, especially when there is a note of appreciation attached, signed by parents and child. Thoughtfulness and genuine gratitude are the keys to this skill, not expense or time.

Allies are not viewed as ridiculous or oversolicitous. In fact, allies enjoy acceptance, approval, psychological and academic benefits for their children. Verbal declarations of an ally position are not as plausible to school personnel as actual concrete expressions of support such as remembering birthdays, teacher work days, holidays, and other important teacher/school-related occasions.

A soundly established ally position creates a comfortable working relationship for future problem-solving encounters, which is, in fact, the key ingredient for effective educational planning and child representation. Ally-to-ally conversations tend to be more cohesive and constructive than opponent-to-opponent debates. The fruits of these discussions remain sweeter for years to come than the bitter aftertaste of confrontations.

If a parent wants to maintain "interest-bearing interpersonal school relationships," an ally position should be well established prior to attempting constructive criticism of school personnel, curricula, policy and procedures, or extra-curricular activities.

SUMMARY

ENROLLMENT GOALS: TO BAG AN EAGLE.

TO BUILD THE BASIS FOR A POSITIVE, CONSTRUCTIVE SCHOOL RELATIONSHIP.

Initial Enrollment Secrets

Secret # 1: No matter what you are told, you can exert some control over the teacher selection process, particularly during the initial enrollment procedure.

Secret # 2: The school administration, faculty, and office staff know who are the most dedicated, talented educators within their facility, and they *do* make strategic placements.

Secret # 3: Your children can be subtly punished if you or they disturb the school personnel's "weather conditions."

Skills for Successful Enrollment: Setting yourself apart from the crowd

Skill # 1: Make a pre-enrollment appointment with the school administrator several days prior to official enrollment.

Skill # 2: Build a positive relationship with the office staff.

Skill # 3: Dress in a businesslike manner.

Skill # 4: Demonstrate a sincere interest in school concerns.

Skill # 5: Offer supportive comments that communicate an appreciation for school and administrative issues.

Skill # 6: Make brief, positive comments about your child.

Skill # 7: Develop a creative "I care about education" kit.

Skill # 8: Give notice of future visibility.

Skill # 9: Notify appropriate school personnel orally and in writing of all health concerns and/or other critical potential problems.

Skill # 10: Cultivate an "ally position."

REMEMBER: Appropriate behavior, appearance, and timing, and a positive, affirmative manner, remove you and your child from the crowd. *Take the randomness out of teacher-assignment.*

MOVING FORWARD . . .

The methodical and effective use of the enrollment skills addressed in this chapter will prevent many possible future problems at school. The next chapter will help parents gain the necessary confidence to represent their children well when a parent/school conference is scheduled to resolve a problem.

3

The Dreaded Parent-Teacher Conference: You Both Win or Your Child Loses

Conferences, ouch! Parents tend to dread conferences with school personnel and often for good reason. Conferences are frequently arranged to discuss problems, not extol virtues; both parties may feel defensive and uncomfortable; the parent, who is on the teacher's "turf," doesn't know the terrain very well and feels at a disadvantage. These natural anxieties can be controlled, however, and even turned into an advantage. They will cause the concerned Child Advocate/Representative to carefully plan and prepare. The discomfort and fearful anticipation will serve as nagging reminders that the first step is to *master your own emotions* by seeking to understand their source.

With understanding we gain knowledge. With knowledge we gain confidence. With confidence we gain a measure of control and advantage in any endeavor, especially one involving interpersonal exchange. Conveniently ignoring the vital educational and social importance to your child of your learning to effectively and successfully communicate with school personnel, only reinforces and perpetuates "school conference phobias." To fully appreciate the interpersonal complexity of parent-school conferences, we will begin by exploring typical reactions of teachers and parents to conference situations.

Parents have often privately expressed to me several fears of conferences. Below I've listed in capsulized version a few representative samples of these comments.

• Trained professionals are better educated than I am, and I will feel insignificant and out of control.

• That conference made me feel outnumbered. There was only one of me and many people from the school system. If so many from the school and county needed to attend a conference about my child, then my child must have very serious problems that I don't really understand. The conference was overwhelming. I wanted to ask questions, but I thought they would sound ignorant. Now, I don't know what to do.

• I'm afraid that I will be blamed for my child's problems. Secretly, I suppose I do fear the problems are my fault. I've tried to be a good parent, but I feel so inadequate, and the conference situation makes me feel like a terrible failure as a parent.

• I never feel prepared for a conference. I really don't know what to do or how to begin. So I seem to be allowing each conference to conclude in a direction not of my own choosing. I hope they know what they're doing. I certainly don't.

• While I'm unfamiliar with the education profession, I'm an educated professional in my own field. I'm not afraid to ask questions until I understand. But I dread dealing with difficult teachers and principals. I may achieve my original goal, but I antagonize and alienate everyone in the process. I'm afraid they will take out their anger on my child.

These quite normal feelings of inadequacy, fear, dread, insignificance, lack of control, and failure (real or imagined) can promote defensive, hostile, apathetic, passive, or aggressive parental behavior. Even total conference avoidance can result from these "school conference phobias" (defined here as: *a persistent, illogical aversion or fear of school conferences which negatively affects one's ability to function adequately as an EP-A/R*).

To provide the best possible representative services for your child, it is not only critical to identify/confront your particular anxieties and discomforts, but also to recognize that teachers suffer from similar kinds of conference dreads and inadequacies. Henry Becker and Joyce Epstein reported in a 1982 school-parent involvement survey, ". . . many teachers do not know how to initiate and accomplish the programs of parent involvement that would help them most . . . Teachers have not been educated in the management of parent involvement . . ."

They also reported that teachers reinforced common stereotypes of parents, such as "pushy upper-middle class parents, helpful middle class parents, and incapable lower class parents." Yet, the teacher solicitation of parent involvement was essentially equally lacking with both educated and uneducated parents. My personal and professional experience is certainly consistent with these findings, which suggest that, in general, teachers often prefer to have minimal contact with parents. Since parental involvement is an invaluable asset in educating children, the most reasonable explanation for the teachers' attitudes would seem to be their own anxieties and insecurities.

Not only do many teachers lack conference skills and parent-involvement program training, but they also have been known to take action to eliminate parent involvement if it becomes threatening or nonsupportive. Susan E. Staub, director of Concerned Educators Against Forced Unionism, reports that in Ohio, National Education Association officials "demanded that the P be taken out of the PTA because that group would not support the union's heavy-handed coercive tactics." While parent involvement is rarely so openly and aggressively repudiated, far too great a number of teachers opt for the "let's not encourage them" method.

Add the teacher's anxieties and insecurities over confrontation to those that parents feel, and suddenly the interpersonal dynamics of the conference have potential to distort and negate positive action/direction for the best interest of the child. The dreaded conference *must* be controlled, and you're probably the one to get this accomplished. This chapter will expand your knowledge, and thus your confidence, and provide you with skills to ensure that your conferring with school personnel will produce mutually beneficial results.

CONFERENCE GOAL: TO DEVELOP IN SCHOOL PERSONNEL A POSITIVE PERCEPTION OF YOUR CHILD.

Regardless of the problem(s) or special program(s) involved, you must encourage the staff to view your child as a capable, likeable achiever who is able, with their support, to cope with difficulties.

▷ **Secret # 1: The parent-school conference is one of your best means of exerting subtle control over teacher attitudes/behavior.**

Many studies about the effects of teacher attitudes toward students indicate that the teacher's attitude toward the student is a powerful factor in grade determination and student success. Wynona Winn, the first woman in Oklahoma's history to be appointed as Superintendent of Schools, and Alfred P. Wilson, professor of Education at Kansas State University, conducted extensive research concerning grouping children according to their academic abilities and the effects of such groupings on instruction. Their findings concluded that upper ability students received more empathy and praise, had more of their ideas used in discussion, and received less direction and less criticism than students in the lower groups. Numerous other studies reported by Winn and Wilson indicated that teachers spend more time with pupils for whom they have higher expectations and that teachers offer more verbal and nonverbal cues such as warmth, verbal affirmation, smiles, and praise to students of higher ability.

In other words, if the teacher views your child as capable, intelligent, and pleasant, then your child reaps the rewards of these positively reinforcing attitudes. Should the teacher view your child as slow, of limited ability, or a discipline problem, he will suffer the consequences.

It is essential that you do everything within your control to develop the appropriate teacher attitude. The parent-teacher conference is your best opportunity to do this.

▷ **Secret #2: Educators often lack the training and skills to conduct beneficially effective conferences.**
It may be up to you to take the lead.

▷ **Secret #3: Parents, teachers, and administrators have many conference dreads in common.**
The first step in successful conference-coping is for you to view the teacher as an ordinary person who probably has the unfortunate but common anxieties and insecurities related to confrontation that anyone else might have. When people perceive a potential threat, they develop defensive postures. You can take the initiative to defuse the "threat factor" by assuming a manner which will encourage open communication.

SKILLS FOR CONTROLLING THE OUTCOME OF THE PARENT-TEACHER CONFERENCE

▶ **Skill #1: "Know thyself."**
Long ago, Socrates suggested to his friends that "knowing oneself is the beginning of wisdom." It still is. Your "self" is the best EP-A/R your child has. Sharpen your sensitivities to

your own feelings and responses, especially those which are *defensive*. Suppose your son's teacher reported, "John didn't complete his homework last week," and you heard yourself respond, "Well, why didn't you call me and tell me about it sooner?" What lay behind your retort? You allowed yourself to take a defensive posture as if you had somehow been made vulnerable by the receipt of this information. Your real message came through loud and clear: "It's not my fault!" That's true, but what has it to do with helping your son? Communication suffered.

Suppose the teacher had said, "John's just lazy; he didn't do his homework again this week." Now you could probably get a majority vote of parents who would agree that you have a right to be angry. Labeling children is inappropriate teacher behavior. But we're not discussing who is right; we are developing strategy. You must *identify your feelings and control your responses* in both situations. *Everything is information to be processed and used,* even feelings, yours and those of the teacher. In the first example, your defensiveness told you something about your own insecurity and maybe even guilt. Your reaction was inappropriate to the stimulus. Seek the source of that feeling and attempt to neutralize it. In the second illustration the teacher's label "lazy" was unskilled and a legitimate cause for your irritation, but, more importantly, it gave you information about her attitude toward John. That information now provides you with a definite goal in your future dealings with this person. You will consciously seek to modify that attitude over a period of time. *To allow defensive emotions—yours or the teacher's—to dominate the mood of a conference is to lose control over its outcome!*

The more knowledge you have about your personal sensitivities, the more able you are to control your reactions and situations affecting your child's school life. Know thyself, but self-knowledge must be properly interpreted or it may lead to a destructive self-image. We must also learn to be generous with ourselves. *Increased self-awareness is growth* and, as such, should be an occasion for solid satisfaction—not grief at discovering yet another flaw in a self that we unrealistically demand should be perfect. As you read this book, you may discover that you have made some mistakes in your past dealings with school personnel. Negative self-images cause us to feel "dumb" as we admit these errors. *Wrong!* Erase that message! Wallowing in past mistakes is destructive. We are all in the process of growing, of becoming. No one comes ready-made. *Identify your mistakes, correct them, flow with it, and smile.* Your children are going to provide you with many more opportunities to grow before it's over.

▶ **Skill # 2: Overcome feelings of intimidation.**

Viewing teachers and administrators as people with families, jobs, and problems just like yours will aid open communications. Mentally elevating them to a level of superiority only prevents you from being effective. Hopefully, they are professionally trained individuals who can provide you with more data about your child than you could gain alone. Superiority is not an issue. The goal is to get people working together, each with his special abilities, to further a child's growth and development.

▶ **Skill # 3: Reduce the interpersonal threat factor by "saving the teacher's face."**

Generally, the term *face-saving* implies a self-generated behavior designed to protect one's own image or self-esteem. I am suggesting a conscious effort on your part to protect the "face" of someone else, your child's teacher, by gracefully permitting the teacher the right to be human and to err. When mistakes occasionally occur that are not harmful to your child, deal with them in such a way that the teacher feels neither embarrassed nor criticized.

Few parents, in my experience, know how to use this technique in their child's best interest. For example, an overly aggressive, highly critical parent might get very angry about a teacher error on a corrected homework assignment. The teacher may have inadvertently marked an item wrong which was actually correct. The parent will usually react with a heated letter to the teacher, an irate telephone call to the principal, or a demand for a conference. This "gotchya" response will alienate the teacher and other staff members. Continued behavior of this nature may result in conscious or subconscious negative attitudes and behaviors toward the child. It would have been much better for all concerned if the parent had actively protected the teacher's "face." For example, a simple polite note might have been directed to the teacher saying something to the effect: "Thank you for so conscientiously grading and sending home John's homework. We are glad John enjoys your class. On the most recent homework assignment, I thought that Item #3 was correct rather than incorrect. Could you help me out with this one? Thanks again."

Allowing individuals to "save face"—not nailing them with their minor errors—while still achieving an identified goal is a true interpersonal art that few achieve. Protecting a teacher's image and self-esteem during conferences will be appreciated and add to your child's interpersonal interest-bearing account.

▶ **Skill #4: Plan your EP-A/R conference profile.**

After years of experience with parents, teachers, administrators, interested community agencies, and family members, I have developed a "Parent Conference Profile" which, if you employ it, will predictably enhance the impressions of you and your family held by school personnel.

PARENT CONFERENCE PROFILE

Demeanor	*Dress*
Calm	Businesslike attire
Direct	Well-groomed
Good listener	
Good eye contact	

Demeanor	Dress
Confident	
Articulate	
Pleasant	
Friendly	
Demonstrates confidence in child	
Demonstrates parental love	
Nonthreatening posture	
Objective approach to issues	

▶ Skill #5: Be prepared

Tips for Getting Ready for Parent-Teacher Conferences

1. Should you feel the need to initiate a conference, call for an appointment. Invite all those at the school who work with your child that you believe might be involved with the issue of concern.

2. If you are requested to attend a scheduled appointment with the school and/or county staff, get all the pertinent data. Make sure you know the exact date, time, and location of the conference. Ask who will be attending the conference and request their titles. Be certain that you understand the reason for the attendance of each professional invited.

3. *Always have a clear perception of the purpose of the conference.* This will aid in the preparation of pertinent questions. If the purpose is not completely clear, call the individual scheduling the conference and ask questions until it becomes clear.

4. *Make a complete list of your questions/concerns.* Often during a conference parents become involved with the discussion and later remember things that they wish they had asked while the entire professional group was present. A list of questions relevant to the purpose of the conference is helpful

and usually accepted well by professionals. No question is unimportant when considering educational planning for your child. Do not be concerned about appearing foolish.

5. *Ask about the approximate length of the conference.* This information will aid you in planning the best use of valuable time with professionals.

6. *Develop a posture of confidence before attending the conference.* This will require much effort and practice for some and little or none for others. If it is an effort, don't fight it: Rehearse!

7. Parents are asked to make many decisions during conferences. *Review at home possible alternative decisions which might be discussed at the conference.* Strive to remain open to many alternatives until you have thoroughly examined all options which might effectively address the issue(s) of concern.

8. *If programs outside of the regular classroom instruction are being considered, decide in advance of the conference to request an opportunity to visit the specific instructional program(s) recommended by the professional staff before signing your approval.* Make a decision about program placement after your visit(s) based upon knowledge gained through firsthand experience, conference information, objective data collected on Forms A and D in Chapter 8, and an appreciation for your child's needs and interests.

9. *Assess your own attitudes and conference philosophy beforehand* in order to provide your child with the best possible representation at the conference. Ask yourself,

DO I BELIEVE THAT MY CHILD CAN:

- Learn and achieve?
- Overcome routine childhood difficulties?
- Cope with normal childhood problems (with adult guidance)?
- Creatively enjoy success and new experiences?

- Make mistakes without fear and accept them as a natural part of daily life and growth?
- Potentially fulfill her personal and vocational goals?
- Be flexible and accept change?
- Enjoy the company of other children and adults?
- Follow reasonable behavioral expectations at school?
- Be happy with and well-adjusted in an acceptable school environment?

At present you may not believe that your child has integrated all of the above ten items into her personality. But it is important that you believe that she has the potential to achieve them with supportive appropriate adult assistance.

DO I BELIEVE THAT I CAN:

- Project a sincere attitude of parental love, affection, and respect?
- Control the conference by focusing on constructive problem-solving directions for conversation?
- Listen for understanding which promotes relevant questions leading to more information and better decision-making for future educational planning?
- Reasonably evaluate the interests and needs of my child?
- Dedicate part of my lifetime parenting responsibilities to learning and improving conference skills which will help to ensure a better education for my child?
- Identify and overcome my own "school-conference phobias"?
- Promote open, nonjudgmental communication?
- Effectively and with a positive posture teach school personnel appropriate and acceptable behaviors toward me and my child?
- Practice and prepare for any conference situation?
- Analyze the quality of my child's education and, thereby, play an active role in educational planning (using Form E in Chapter 8)?

If you can answer yes to these two sets of questions, you are ready for any conference situation, no matter how difficult. If some of these goals are still beyond your reach, press on. The whole purpose of this book is to help you improve your skills in representing your child and planning his/her educational journey.

▶ **Skill #6: Relax during a conference, especially at the beginning.**

Generally speaking, teachers enjoy talking. Focus on positive statements about the school. Your sincerely expressed comments set the mood for their future dealings with you. These are warm-up exercises letting everyone know that you are a pleasant, constructive individual.

▶ **Skill #7: Facilitate an understanding of your child's home environment.**

Openly discuss family issues of relevance to the purpose of the conference.

▶ **Skill #8: Express interest in communicating with all school personnel,** particularly those people who work with your child.

▶ **Skill #9: Relate something positive about your child, but balance the comments.**

Don't babble on about his/her wonderful accomplishments since five months of age. Do say: "He loves to learn new things." "She has always been a bright child." "He loves to paint." "She enjoys outdoors and camping."

▶ **Skill #10: Encourage information about your child's successes in school.**

All too often school personnel focus on children's unsuccessful academic and social behaviors. To inquire, simply ask something such as, "I'm very interested in my child's educational progress. Could you tell me about some of his successful academic and social experiences?" Usually you'll be pleasantly surprised at the positive responses. Occasionally, the teacher will continue to focus on negative issues. Listen patiently, say "Thank you," and repeat your original question about successful experiences. Communicate that you want to see the whole picture. In this manner, the conference remains in your control. You have remained calm and maintained a nonthreatening profile. While you will need to discuss problems, there are appropriate terms and language patterns to use which will cause teachers to think more positively even about the problems.

Usually it is totally unnecessary to inquire about difficulties your child is having. Rarely is a conference requested purely to tell a parent about the excellent progress of a child. Therefore, focus on the positive throughout the entire conference. In effect, you will be teaching the school staff acceptable behaviors toward you and your child. The conference example on page 69 demonstrates how to maintain a positive posture in spite of uncomfortable, irritating, or frightening information about your child.

▶ **Skill # 11: Believe that your child is capable of achieving!**

If you don't, the teacher probably won't and neither will your child. Viewing your child as a winner, as capable and responsible, is the best profile for a Child Advocate/Representative. Unfortunately, many parents do not view themselves or their children as winners, achievers, who possess dignity and character; therefore, they are unable to project this image during the dreaded conference. If you can't profoundly believe your child is special and capable, then at least recognize that as a responsible parent and representative you owe him the best educational opportunities available. Maintain a profile which exudes realistic confidence in your child's potential if not delight in his present achievements.

It is unlikely that anyone else will perceive your child as capable if you don't. You're probably creating an unintentional but nevertheless self-defeating series of school experiences for him if you neglect to support him in positive, constructive ways during the conference.

Support should not be interpreted as rationalizing or excusing inappropriate behaviors. Support is defined here as demonstrating genuine respect and concern for your child's abilities and rights. If consequences for unacceptable behavior are necessary, then your support will reflect an objective, reasonable, kind, and judicious verdict. The child's character and person will not be challenged.

▶ **Skill # 12: If it is necessary to relate unfortunate, negative past experiences, conclude your conversation with constructive action and positive direction taken to assist her in coping with the consequences.**

Whatever the problem (for example, if your child was sexually molested), be supportive and view her as capable of overcoming it and putting unfortunate experiences in the past.

▶ **Skill # 13:**
Direct your conference time toward constructive action and effective solutions which are critical to the mental, physical, and educational well-being of your child. Approximately 75 percent of the conference conversation should focus on action, constructive progress, time management for accomplishing objectives, and redefining the school program. Only 25 percent of conference time should be spent on the review of the actual problems.

This suggested time allocation is intended to give you an opportunity to consider the importance of other demands upon the time of the professional staff and your own schedule, particularly if you work outside of the home. Time is precious and using it wisely will contribute to the success of each conference.

Some health, emotional, social, or academic problems are so severe that a long, hard review of the specifics is essential for effective decision-making. Instead of one long conference, a series of conferences may be scheduled to review these cases. Again, conference time management still remains a critical consideration. Nonproductive time expenditure costs everyone, especially the child.

▶ **Skill # 14: Give everyone present at the conference an opportunity to speak.**

The typical parent/one-teacher conference is becoming rarer with each educational innovation. The advent of differentiated staffing, team teaching, departmentalization, team leaders, master teachers, curriculum specialists, and guidance counselors has dictated that most conferences will involve many professionals and usually one parent. Often one person will conduct the conference and prepare the setting. However, remember that you are in control. Everyone who contributes must seek to communicate with you. Maintain a calm, positive, persistent manner. Notice if everyone gets to speak. If not, when an appropriate opportunity presents itself, ask those who haven't spoken for their comments. Simply ask, "Do you have any comments you would like to make about my child?" Then listen to the first few sentences very carefully. Professionals have been trained to strive conscientiously to begin with positive child-centered statements. If the professional neglects to do this and immediately begins with a negative, perhaps you need to evaluate the relative value of the time your child spends with this individual.

▶ **Skill # 15:**
Use a constructive, positive, problem-solving, "Get-down-to-business and let's-progress" manner to teach the school staff how you and your child wish to be treated. This will also set the tone for future meetings.

▶ **Skill # 16: Conclude all academically oriented conferences with a clear understanding of future educational goals and specific instructional objectives for your child.**

This is not difficult. Just ask, "What are the immediate instructional goals for my child? Will they be easily accomplished? How may I help? What are the long-range instructional objectives? Do you expect her to achieve these skills/objectives/goals? If not, why not? If so, what is a reasonable time period in which to expect achievement of the designated goals?"

CONFERENCE EXAMPLE: WHAT TO DO IF THE TEACHER SEES THE NEGATIVE AND THE PARENT SEEKS TO SOLVE!

MARGINAL TEACHER: Fred is disruptive in class. He talks constantly and never finishes his work. When I ask him to get busy, he just sits there playing with his crayons or pencils.

PARENT: I can see that you're concerned about Fred's wasting his valuable learning opportunities. May I see the work that was incomplete?

TEACHER: Here is a stack from two weeks' worth of work. See how I had to grade him. All papers earned an "F."

PARENT: Fred has much potential and is capable. Yet, he certainly has not performed well on these tasks. At home he is motivated to complete tasks because he enjoys a particular TV show. He's allowed to see the show when he accomplishes assignments. Of course, because he's only eight years old, we make sure that the tasks are those he can successfully complete. Do you think Fred is capable of successfully completing the work you have assigned?

TEACHER: He's capable, just lazy.

PARENT: Yes, you're right. He is capable. He is industrious at home and in his Boy Scout troup. I'm glad that you know how capable he is.

TEACHER: But he is lazy.

PARENT: Well, with a child this age there could be so many reasons he isn't completing his assignments. We don't have any real problems at home right now. Can you help me think of several possible reasons for incomplete work?

TEACHER: I would like to help. That's why I asked you to come in for a conference. It does seem that Fred has had many additional assignments the last two weeks because of the science fair projects and social studies displays. He also seems to enjoy the new student, Todd, who enrolled recently.

PARENT: Do you think that Fred is distracted by the new student? Knowing the way Fred likes to make friends, I imagine he occasionally distracts the new student.

TEACHER: They do seem to get along well. They eat lunch together and sit beside one another during class.

PARENT: I appreciate the interest and care you show for Fred. Would it be helpful to send incomplete work home at the end of the day so that I can discuss it with Fred and follow up?

TEACHER: Yes, I would be happy to do that. It would be helpful. I will also reassign classroom seating. Perhaps separating Fred from his new-found friend would make it possible for both of them to complete their class assignments.

PARENT: I would like to make a tentative appointment to visit the classroom during an instructional time. If our decisions to change the seating arrangement and send incomplete work home don't help him improve, then I'll keep the appointment. Because I know Fred so well, perhaps I can help to determine other reasons why he isn't finishing his work. If the changes help, then a visit may not be necessary. Whatever happens, I'm certain that you and I and Fred can overcome this temporary problem. He will be back on track soon because he is so capable. Thank you again for your time and concern.

HOW DID THIS PARENT RATE AS A CHILD ADVOCATE/REPRESENTATIVE?

1. The parent never acknowledged the child as "lazy." A label with negative connotations such as "lazy" has no room in a conference conversation. As your child's representative, do not waste time on words that focus the teacher's attention away from the capable-child profile you're trying to develop. Acceptance of such terminology reinforces the teacher's current view of your child and is detrimental to effective analysis of the issues and, therefore, a constructive solution. Analysis of a child's difficulties is totally different from attaching labels to his personality.

2. The parent constantly referred to the child's time, learning opportunities, and responsibilities in the resolution of the problem. The main purpose of the conference is not to help the teacher but to help the child. Occasionally it is necessary to subtly remind teachers that it is a child-centered conference. While the teacher's needs are important, they are of secondary consideration.

3. Objective evidence was discussed (e.g., seating arrangement, incomplete work, age, new student, recent projects) and became the focus of problem-solving planning.

4. Family value statements were peppered throughout the conference (e.g., "Fred likes to make friends"). Family values are communicated in many ways: dress, attitude, demeanor, and indirect or direct value statements. These expressions of family values leave school personnel with indelible impressions.

5. The parent did not ignore the problem. The problem was approached as a completely natural situation in childhood. Constructive goals were stated, and a team effort (teacher, parent, and child) consolidated.

6. The conference was summarized by clearly defining future action. Every conference should conclude with well-established goals and plans for their implementation.

7. The parent concluded with a brief, uneffusive statement of appreciation. Positive working relations are more easily developed when the school staff believes they are genuinely appreciated.

For the sake of a vivid depiction of positive parental control, this conference example has exaggerated overtones of "pushy positives." Nonetheless, it clearly represents a very real and viable means of control without conflict during confrontation, and ultimately the parent's goals are achieved. This parent earns an "A" as an A/R.

To illustrate the conversational skills which keep the marginal teacher focused upon a capable image of your child, I elected to use the "lazy child syndrome" in this example because so many marginal teachers complain of "lazy but capable" children. This is a common "one-on-one" parent-teacher conference issue, but one which can be meaningfully directed toward a problem-solving mode.

You may think I'm unrealistic when I say that I've never seen a lazy child. I've only seen children who were not motivated because of a variety of factors. We adults procrastinate when we want to avoid unfulfilling tasks or tasks where we fear failure, lack of appreciation, or lack of reward. Children experience this in "megaform." The powerful adults have demanded that unfulfilling tasks be completed every day, on a specific time schedule, with few rewards. Any resistance is easily labeled "lazy." If we want children to work energetically, the key then is to make the tasks fulfilling and/or rewarding to complete. Feelings of achievement and success for completing difficult and demanding tasks are the best kinds of rewards. Skilled teachers know this and use the powerful feeling of success to motivate children.

The dreaded parent-teacher conference can be a satisfying experience when it concludes with positive direction for future action, a comfortable relationship with school personnel, and, most importantly, when all involved maintain a mental image of your child as capable of overcoming problems and achieving identified goals and, generally, as a special human being.

There is truly no need to fear conferences when you have accomplished the skills which put you in control of the outcome. You can see that you do not need to have a degree in education to guide school personnel to work with your child in caring, humane, educationally excellent ways. Simply project an attitude of confidence that your child is an achiever, a winner, a coper. It's likely they will do the same. Ultimately, think of the long-range ripple effect of your child's believing that she is a winner, a coper, an achiever, a nice person, loved and respected.

Now isn't learning conference skills worth a few hours of your time? Practice, practice, practice! Practice conference skills at home. Have a friend or your spouse role-play with you, assuming the teacher role(s) and giving you a rehearsal before you go to the appointed conference. Practice until you're comfortable delivering positive, child-centered statements.

SOME CONFERENCE DO'S AND DON'TS

1. *Do not do all of the talking.* All members of the group want to talk and can add to your decision-making data.

2. *Be a good listener.* Pay attention to all statements. Ask short questions that will encourage more participation by

members of the group. Be eager to understand other points of view and to clarify your own. You might begin by saying, "I wonder if. . . ," or "What do you think about. . . ," or "What would happen if . . ."

3. *Do not argue.* Permit group members to express their thoughts. You express yours. Strive to mutually understand each other's position. There often is far more agreement than difference. Or you may find the other party is right. But do not agree just to be agreeable. There is too much at stake. And even if you disagree, acknowledge your understanding of the other position. It's okay to thoroughly understand and still totally disagree.

4. *Do not interrupt.* Even if you disagree, it is an interpersonal error to interrupt, showing disregard for another's thoughts. Interruptions tend to prevent positive interaction. If you are interrupted, continue calmly talking until you have completed your thought.

5. *Ask relevant questions* that add to your data for more informed decision-making. Ask questions that will encourage the members of the group to disclose their attitudes about your child, their plans for future academic and social goals and objectives for your child.

6. *Restate, in your own words, your understanding of everything that all parties said until all agree upon the same conference interpretation.* This helps you and the group see the issues clearly. It also helps you become a part of the group, more than a mere outsider. When you work to clarify and understand all members' positions, you set the stage to present your thoughts. The group is more likely to perceive what you have to say in a positive light.

7. *Do not digress from the purpose of the conference.* Concentrate on central issues. Issues irrelevant to the conference can be postponed for future discussion.

8. *Admit parenting errors if they are relevant to conference issues.* It's okay—there are no parents, teachers, or ad-

ministrators whose records are free of occasional mistakes.

9. *Make sure all conferences translate into future action.* Ask how you will be able to monitor the progress of the implementation of the plan.

10. *Be satisfied with appropriate progress and improvements.* Sudden improvements do occur as a result of conferences; however, small gains are usually the norm. *Be dissatisfied with no progress,* and seek further conferences to decide upon other action.

11. *Follow up each conference with a thank-you note to the primary person conducting it;* that may be the guidance counselor, teacher, or principal. Take that opportunity to tell her specifically when you'll follow-up and inquire about your child's progress as a result of the plans conceived. This demonstrates your sincere appreciation, your genuine interest in concrete results, and your respect for the conferencing process. Just a few minutes for a brief note can produce daily benefits for your child.

SUMMARY

CONFERENCE GOAL: TO CONTINUALLY DEVELOP THE ATTITUDES OF THE SCHOOL STAFF TOWARD YOUR CHILD SO THAT THEY PERCEIVE HIM AS CAPABLE OF ACHIEVING, COPING, AND BECOMING A LIKEABLE, SUCCESSFUL PERSON.

Conference Secrets:

Secret #1: The parent-school conference is one of your best means of exerting subtle control over teacher attitudes/behavior.

Secret #2: Educators often lack the training and skills to conduct effective conferences.

Secret #3: Parents, teachers, and administrators have many conference dreads and phobias in common.

Conference Skills:

Skill # 1: Identify personal secret sensitivities which cause you to feel threatened, fearful, or uncomfortable, and control your responses.

Skill # 2: Accept that teachers share similar kinds of conference fears and feelings. This will help alleviate some of your fears and aid open communication.

Skill # 3: Minimize interpersonal threat factors by generously helping the teacher to save face.

Skill # 4: Review the "parent conference profile" and adopt those behaviors that will work well for you.

Skill # 5: Be prepared! Review conference preparation tips.

Skill # 6: Relax during a conference, especially at the beginning.

Skill # 7: Facilitate an understanding of your child's home environment.

Skill # 8: Express interest in communication with all school personnel.

Skill # 9: Relate something positive about your child.

Skill # 10: Encourage information about your child's successes in school.

Skill # 11: Believe that your child is capable of achieving.

Skill # 12: When it is necessary to relate unfortunate past experiences, conclude the conversation with a discussion about the constructive action taken to help your child cope.

Skill # 13: Direct the conference time meaningfully toward constructive future action.

Skill # 14: Give everyone present an opportunity to speak.

Skill # 15: Use a "get-down-to-business and let's-progress" manner.

Skill # 16: Conclude all conferences with a clear understanding of future educational goals and specific instructional objectives.

REMEMBER: Attack the problem and not the child. Avoid characterizing and labeling. Analyze the difficulties and alternative resolutions. Practice, practice, practice! Advocate/Representative and Education Planner roles may be demanding and difficult, but practice will produce confidence and proficiency.

MOVING FORWARD . . .

Now that you are aware of the secrets involved in conference dynamics and have practiced the skills which make them successful, we're ready to discuss a key problem that many parents confront. What do you do when you are dissatisfied with your child's teacher, and you would like to have him reassigned? Your child has a buzzard and you want an eagle. The next chapter can help you successfully achieve reassignment with minimal friction.

4
Confrontation Without Conflict: When the Teacher Is the Problem

Public school teaching is among the lowest paying professions. We should not be surprised then that it usually doesn't attract the higher-ability college students. Increasing numbers of potential eagles are not choosing education as a career; subsequently our buzzard population is likely to grow over the next decade. Tragically, the reform that is desperately needed now will not occur soon enough to help your elementary-age child.

Principals report that between 5 and 15 percent of their faculties are unqualified to teach. If this is true, why have only eighty-six tenured teachers been dismissed for incompetence during the past forty-three years in the entire nation? Answer: The legal definition of competence and the rules of evidence make it highly unlikely that a charge of incompetence would be upheld in court.

Because trained administrators, school boards, and skilled attorneys struggle to little avail with the competence issue, I recommend that you direct your concerns not to teacher competence but to *teacher acceptability for your individual child.* A teacher could be highly competent with all other children and still be unacceptable for your child. Focus upon the acceptability of the teacher and not the competence.

Dale Carnegie said, "When dealing with people, remember you are not dealing with creatures of logic, but with creatures of emotion, creatures bristling with prejudice and motivated by pride and vanity." Teachers and parents alike suffer from these human conditions which Mr. Carnegie describes so well.

Finding appropriate criteria by which to evaluate the teacher's acceptability for your child is a demanding task and must be done with finesse and objectivity.

I've seen parents attempt to effect the reassignment of their children for totally unsound reasons. Wounded egos and illogical, inadequate planning hindered them from maximum child representation and reasonably effective decision-making. For example, a talented, creative, humanistic, and skilled second grade teacher was interrupted during class instruction by a parent demanding an immediate appointment. The teacher explained that she was working with the children at the present time but would be happy to schedule a future appointment.

The parent was angry because the teacher would not leave her class and meet with her. She went to the principal and demanded that her son Bob be removed from that "terrible, rude" teacher's class.

After the principal explained to the teacher the parent's request, the teacher said that she was accustomed to parents who wanted their children in her room and would be amenable to the new classroom assignment.

Bob was reassigned to a teacher who habitually verbally and physically abused students. The mother ruined the child's second grade experience because she didn't take planned, specific measures to determine the teacher's acceptability for her child prior to making a request for reassignment. She never visited either of the teachers' classrooms during instruction.

"Acceptability" is a delicate issue because teachers have different levels of competence in subject areas, grade levels, classroom management, and instructional delivery methods, and different levels of sensitivity to children's developmental physical and emotional needs.

Form A on page 185 in Chapter 8 will help you answer the question "Is the teacher acceptable for my child?" This form will also enhance your objectivity, which promotes logical decisions and deters emotion-laden, prejudicial thinking. Parents should not decide that a teacher is unacceptable for their child and request reassignment without thorough deliberation.

REASSIGNMENT GOAL # 1: TO HAVE AN ACCEPTABLE TEACHER ASSIGNED TO YOUR CHILD WITHOUT ALIENATING SCHOOL PERSONNEL.

Seek precedent in your child's school. Some principals accede as a matter of policy to all such requests. If you find this so in your school, your problem is solved. Chances are, however, it will not be quite so simple.

REASSIGNMENT GOAL # 2: TO PROVIDE FOR A SMOOTH CLASSROOM TRANSITION WITHOUT CONFLICT.

REASSIGNMENT GOAL # 3: TO CONTINUE TO ENSURE POSITIVE SCHOOL RELATIONSHIPS FOR YOUR CHILD.

▷ **Secret # 1: School administrators are usually reluctant to move a child from an unacceptable teacher's classroom to another classroom.**

If one parent request is honored, the administrator becomes concerned about setting a precedent. In effect, reassigning one child creates many more potential decision-making problems for the administrator.

In many cases you won't be the only parent who has requested that a child be removed from that teacher's classroom. If the administrator knows the teacher to be unacceptable and that there is a history of prior parent complaints and requests for reassignment from that particular teacher's class, then moving your child to another classroom could cause other parents to become angry that their requests were not honored. Hence, more trouble for the administrator.

A principal's response to your request may lead you to think you're the only parent who has been dissatisfied. This is understandable since it would be "unprofessional" to tell you about other complaints. The teacher's rights must be protected. The question is not whether other parents are satisfied or dissatisfied with the teacher's performance; it is simply, "Is the teacher acceptable for my child?"

If it became a known fact in a school's community of parents that a particular teacher constantly had children removed from his classroom upon the request of parents, then a numbers game could be created.

Class size is equalized for every teacher. Would it be logical or fair to allow an incompetent teacher to have ten students and a superior teacher to be overcrowded with thirty-five students? This community ripple effect of requests for reassignment is, therefore, a concern to the decision-making administrator. Some requests for change are honored, and some are not. Herein lies the challenge for creatively managing and coping with a situation which will allow the administrator to decide to change your child's class assignment without creating future problems for himself within the community.

The morale of the faculty is also of concern. Teachers justifiably lose confidence and respect for an administration that will move children every time a parent is angry and demands a change.

▷ **Secret # 2: Children are reassigned during the school year to other teachers and programs.**

The reasons and methods for reassignment are multidiverse. Even if you have heard that the principal will not reassign students, if you follow proper procedures and apply creative management coping skills, you will probably be successful. Long-range, not temporary, success is the crucial goal. The following story of a "pushy mother" highlights this basic premise:

A well-intentioned but tactless mother believed her child, Alex, to be gifted. She requested that Alex be evaluated for the school's gifted program. Prior to the initial testing, the mother had raised her voice to the guidance counselor and insisted that Alex be tested soon. The mother exhibited no sensitivity to the overall demands upon the counselor, who served many students other than Alex. The counselor told many teachers and the administration how "pushy" and "overbearing" the mother was to her during their conference. The guidance counselor, according to accepted procedure, administered the first test, which was an I.Q. test, to determine if further testing was necessary. Alex's I.Q. test results indicated high average intelligence but not quite high enough to meet state criteria for admittance into the gifted program.

The counselor did not recommend further testing. At this point, the mother went to the principal and maligned the ability of the counselor. Every action taken by the counselor was within the appropriate testing procedures and guidelines. However, I.Q. tests frequently leave some prompting options and judgment calls to the discretion of the professional administering the test. The personalities of the "tester" and "testee" may cause the child to respond incorrectly. Did the counselor's irritation toward the mother affect the test results? The time of day an I.Q. test is administered may also have some effect upon the test results. Did the counselor give the test in the afternoon when the child might have been tired? I.Q. tests can vary as much as ten points on either side of the reported I.Q. results. Given all of these factors and other variables, a "pure I.Q. score" is impossible to obtain.

Alex was tested a few months later by another professional, qualified for further testing, and eventually qualified for and successfully participated in the gifted program.

The mother finally accomplished her goal, but she alienated the counselor, teacher, and administrator because she complained, bullied, and annoyed everyone with her hostile-aggressive behavior. There were more effective means by which to achieve the same goal and remain on friendly terms with all concerned, thereby continuing to enhance Alex's positive relationships at school. The "feeling residue" that she left on deposit with school personnel was basically, "Alex's mother thinks he is gifted. You know she has to prove she's right. I don't think he is gifted. He is just a spoiled brat who gets his way. Eventually she'll see that he can't make it in the gifted program." While the mother may have gotten him in the program by insisting on further testing, if the teacher attitudes are negative about Alex's performance, then subconsciously the teachers involved may try to prove they were right and the mother was wrong about Alex's ability. The mother's goal may be only a temporary accomplishment. Even when test scores validate that Alex is gifted, Alex may experience failure in the program because the teachers perceive him as "not gifted," just a child with a "pushy" mother.

Occasionally several students from different classes are reassigned at the same time. As the following story illustrates, this can present an ideal opportunity to have your child reassigned. In one such instance, a first grade teacher who was competently skilled in classroom management and methods had a tendency to be insensitive about child growth and emotional developmental needs. Often she was severely strict regarding behavior.

A mother of a shy little girl pleaded with the administrator to move her child to another teacher's class because Beth cried every morning before school and hated school because she was afraid of her teacher. The mother said she knew that the teacher was not unkind but was often unreasonable in behavioral expectations. She knew her child's teacher was fine but simply was not the right one for this time in Beth's development.

The administrator was aware of the teacher's many strengths and few weaknesses and mentally (not verbally) agreed with the parent's assessment of the situation. She was also aware of upcoming student reassignments because a new teacher was being hired to alleviate an overcrowded situation. This would be an ideal time to reassign Beth without making it obvious to the community and faculty that a request for class change had been honored.

Knowing that the teacher was already angry with the mother because the mother had initiated a poorly delivered request for change during a parent-teacher conference, the administrator discussed the issue with the teacher. Her immediate response was, "Well I'm not going to give the parent the satisfaction of pushing me around." The administrator directly asked the teacher if she was willing to let this parent literally cry on her doorstep all year and make her life miserable.

The teacher said that if she could let the parent know that she alone had decided that an academic reassignment was needed and that it had nothing to do with the mother's request or the administrator's pressure, then she would want to move the child because she didn't want the mother bothering her.

Knowing the teacher's somewhat abrasive personality, the administrator stated that the teacher could make this decision and inform the mother. The child was reassigned and seemed to have a wonderful first grade experience. The mother, the teacher, and the administrator all accomplished their goals.

This mother had handled the situation with little imagination. She clumsily initiated the request with the teacher, implying criticism of her behavior. Then, when she "botched" up her plan, she went "over the teacher's head" to achieve her goal. Even though her approach to the administrator was calm and reasonable, the damage had been done: a power struggle had been joined. The administrator managed to smooth out the interpersonal problems enough to ultimately help Beth and avoid unnecessary conflict with the teacher. As long as the teacher believed that she would not be embarrassed in front of her colleagues, that she had the decision-making control, and that the parent knew that she, the teacher, was more powerful than the "pushy parent" and was part of the administrative decision-making, then she would decide in favor of reassigning the child. Basically self-interest was the teacher's motivation.

It's unfortunate, but often egos of parents, teachers, and administrators blind them to the needs of the child and the many alternative solutions which might meet those needs. That same "humanness" that causes our blindness can wonderfully surprise us with our own nurturing instincts. And so it is with devoted teachers who come to love their children and want to protect and guide their development. These select few do genuinely care about their students' development even after the children are promoted to the next grade level. I've observed teams of teachers try to arrange student assignments to the succeeding grades so that all of their students would be placed in the superior teachers' classes. They specifically requested that their students not be placed in Ms. X's class because they cared too much about them to see them suffer during the forthcoming school term. With deep conscience they agonized over students assigned to Ms. X's class.

▶ **Skill #1: Obtain a letter from your family physician if possible—this seems to be the easiest and the least conflict-producing means of gaining reassignment.**

If your child appears to be suffering emotionally, mentally, or physically as a result of the classroom environment and a physician is willing to assert that, indeed, such might be a possibility, usually a principal will honor the physician's recommendation for reassignment to a new classroom teacher.

Here are a few examples of this type of creative EP-A/R problem-solving: One parent brought a letter from a physician stating that her child had hives possibly due to stress. The physician wanted to request another classroom situation to determine if it might be school-related stress. The child had complained frequently of fearing school.

Note that the current teacher was not criticized in the physician's letter, nor did he make casual assertions he could not prove. Perhaps there were some students in the classroom who were making it very difficult for the child involved. The letter left the cause of the school fears open-ended. The administrator is now aware of the child's problem; the teacher won't be offended if the reassignment occurs because he has not been identified as the source of the stress. Rather than opponents, the teacher and administrator become partners with the physicians and parents in the research endeavor. But there is also the subtlest of warnings that should they do nothing after having been apprised of a medical suggestion and the condition worsens, they become vulnerable.

Martha was a quiet child who had enjoyed school for several years. In third grade she was assigned to a tough-minded, insensitive teacher who verbally abused her.

The school facility had several portable classrooms positioned quite far away from the large main building which housed most of the student population. There were no covered walkways connecting the portable classrooms to the main facility. When it rained, the children got wet going to scheduled activities such as lunch, music, and the library. Martha was assigned to one of these classrooms.

Martha's mother analyzed the situation and decided to ask

the pediatrician to recommend a room where her child would not have to walk in the rain because Martha had previously had pneumonia and was highly susceptible to inclement weather conditions.

The mother managed to effectively resolve the situation without offending the teacher or the administrator. The child was reassigned in the main building and enjoyed her new teacher. This parent found a genuine and honest means to remove her child from a negative environment without alienating anyone on the professional staff.

Another parent wisely requested to have Anne, her first grader, placed in a classroom close to the clinic because she received several medications each day for asthma attacks. The parent knew that in Anne's grade level, the most outstanding teacher's classroom was the closest to the clinic.

Is this parental behavior in any way exploitatively manipulative? Consider that we manage our jobs, careers, homes, marriages, businesses, and other personal and business relationships in order to fulfill our needs. It is a wise and prudent person who recognizes that managing public school interaction determines the quality of educational programs received.

Creatively managing a problem and resolving that problem with integrity, without harm to anyone, and in the best interest of your child is a productive strategy, a positive experience for all concerned. Exploitative manipulation, on the other hand, usually causes people to feel angry, misused, and mistreated. Apply your EP-A/R energies toward managing situations positively. Creative management of situations is easiest and most effective when applied as preventive measures. It is much more difficult to manage an already existing problem.

When a physician can ethically render assistance, a parent need not complain or report unacceptable teacher performance. Simply and politely call for an appointment with the

school administrator, present the physician's written recommendation, and request reassignment to another classroom.
Thank the administrator for her kind assistance. Follow-up a
few weeks later with a thank-you note and a brief report
about your child's progress as a result of her help. Even this
small expression of appreciation will register in your "interpersonal interest-bearing account." So few parents think to
send thank-you notes to school personnel.

If you cannot justifiably utilize a physician's recommendation to have your child reassigned, then the following skills
may be of help.

▶ **Skill #2: Make an appointment with the school administrator and take a list of written statements which
express constructive, objective concerns about the instructional program.**

This skill is utilized when a parent elects to discuss openly
the possibility that the teacher may be unacceptable to meet
your child's educational needs.

Previously, I implied that "going over the teacher's head"
was generally not the wisest approach to resolving difficulties. However, in some instances you may find it necessary to
talk about your specific concerns with the administration before talking with the classroom teacher. If so, written statements expressing specifics presented calmly and articulately
are more likely to gain the interest and support of the administration than emotional nonspecifics that cannot be verified.

Many helpful examples of relevant material which would
be recognized and respected as genuine concerns for consideration for change in classroom assignment are outlined in
Form A on page 185 and in Form D on page 199.

▶ **Skill #3: Speak in terms of "alternative strategies"
when you discuss classroom reassignment with administrators.**

Alternative strategy is a term occasionally used by professionals to refer to accepted alternative problem-solving techniques that reflect creativity, flexibility, and above all, sound professional judgment. Reassignment is one of many alternative strategies often recommended to help children adjust to the school environment. Teachers are more likely to be amenable to student reassignment if it is proposed as a professional alternative strategy to help a child than if they are asked to deal with their own "unacceptability" as defined by you. If the teachers are more amenable, then the administration is more likely to approve a change of teachers.

Occasionally, teachers assume blame when there is none, and exhibit hostile, defensive behavior which makes it more difficult to achieve your goal of reassignment. The delicate art of requesting the alternative strategy of a new classroom assignment must be carefully planned prior to discussion with the administration. You may want to first propose various less "drastic" or "threatening" changes so as not to seem to be accusing of the teacher. These changes may even solve the problem without your having to resort to reassignment!

Sissy's case illustrates one reason why school personnel decide to reassign students. Sissy was an intelligent, beautiful little girl. Unfortunately, she was severely emotionally handicapped. She physically and mentally abused herself and other children. Because of overcrowded conditions in the EH (Emotionally Handicapped) Program, the county staff asked the school staff to try the alternative strategy of assigning another grade level teacher for Sissy. When the principal informed Sissy's current teacher of this request, she was threatened by the suggestion. She was a new teacher and very concerned about her students and earning the respect of her colleagues. She feared that Sissy's next teacher might not have the problems with Sissy that she was having. She personalized Sissy's problems because of her lack of experience. Yet, she was an excellent teacher.

When Sissy was moved, in only a week she was exhibiting

the same behaviors as before the move. Sissy's former teacher was relieved that she was not going to be blamed as the source of the child's problems.

Teachers occasionally assume blame when there is none, and exhibit hostile, defensive behavior which makes it more difficult to achieve your goal of reassignment. The delicate art of requesting the alternative strategy of a new classroom assignment must be carefully planned prior to discussion with the administration.

For your information, I have listed various possible alternative strategies that are often considered. This list should serve as a guide for parents when they are involved in problem-solving conferences. Certainly all of these strategies are not appropriate for every conference and every child. The selected strategies therefore should be individually prescribed to meet each child's unique needs. After reviewing this list, you may want to discuss with school personnel several strategies other than reassignment which might offer practical solutions to your child's difficulties. The strategies are given in question form to make them more easily adaptable for conference discussion.

CURRICULUM CHANGES:

1. Is the level of academic instruction appropriate? (Your concern here is whether or not your child is being academically challenged, or whether the challenges are so great that failure is a regular experience.)

2. Should the instructional level be made more or less demanding? If so, in what subject areas are instructional level changes necessary?

3. What instructional methods work best for your child? (Does your child learn best by seeing, hearing, or touching, or using a combination of these senses? The school system should have modality tests available to determine the answer to this question. These tests could indicate that a change in

the instructional method is necessary. Ask an administrator or teacher to explain modality testing and the school/district procedures for administering these tests.)

REFERRAL TO SPECIAL PROGRAMS/RESOURCES WITHIN THE SCHOOL

1. What special services are provided which might help resolve your child's problems?
2. Would counseling services be helpful?
3. Is there a supplementary reading program for which your child would qualify? Would it be appropriate to test at this time to determine qualification?
4. Are there peer tutors or volunteers who give special one-to-one help to students?
5. Should a psychologist be consulted?
6. Should a curriculum specialist be consulted?
7. Should a reading specialist be consulted?

CLASSROOM MANAGEMENT

1. Are increased assignments needed? (Is your child bored? Are assignments totally uninteresting and unstimulating?)
2. Should the amount of work required per assignment be decreased? (Does your child feel defeated because of the volume of work assigned?)
3. Is there a need for a change in schedule or classroom teacher? (Does your child talk frequently about his unhappiness over a specific subject(s) or teacher(s)?)
4. Would a different seating arrangement help resolve the difficulties? (Are others distracting your child, or is he distracting them from tasks?)
5. Would a study carrel decrease distractions? (Study carrels—usually a small physical barrier—provide more privacy for those who need fewer distractions in order to concentrate.)

6. Is a reward system used to motivate your child? (Praise is usually an effective motivator with children. Free time, tokens, stars, and prizes are often used to encourage students to do their best. It is my professional opinion that praising, hugging, and other expressions of caring for children and giving them any extra "special" individual attention are the most effective positive reinforcers.)

7. Is there a consistently employed system of consequences for unacceptable behavior? A few frequently utilized disciplinary techniques are:

Time Outs: Temporarily separating a student from his peers.

Spanking (corporal punishment): Legal in some states.

Withholding Privileges: Something with which we parents are familiar.

Assignment to an alternative school: An instructional situation whereby students with severely unacceptable classroom behaviors are prepared to reenter the "regular" school program.

Suspension: Preventing a child from attending school for a brief period of time.

8. Does the guidance counselor work with the class concerning disruptive behavior?

9. Is there a need for increased individual attention?

10. Does the school's administration follow up disciplinary action with positive support to help the child improve behavior?

HELP FROM AGENCIES OUTSIDE THE SCHOOL SYSTEM

1. Should I seek therapy for my child outside of the school's services?

2. Would individual therapy, group therapy, or both be suggested?

3. Should I seek help from a physician?

▶ **Skill # 4:**

Should you elect to request the "alternative strategy" of a new classroom assignment, **be prepared to address several questions which the administration or teacher might ask.**

LIKELY QUESTIONS:

1. Why are you wanting a change?
2. Has the present teacher done something which has caused you to make this request?
3. Is your child having academic or social difficulties which could be resolved by a new classroom assignment?
4. Have you written a formal request?
5. Do you have reason to believe, whatever the problems, that they cannot be resolved in the present classroom situation?

Preparing answers to these sample questions and practicing the conference skills listed in Chapter 3 better prepare parents to plan and implement a request for reassignment.

▶ **Skill # 5: Become aware of the existing conditions in your child's present classroom environment which might be due cause for moving your child.**

Identify specific difficulties your child may have as a result of some of these environmental elements. Even if the teacher is the primary source of your child's lack of educational progress and/or emotional disturbance, strive to discover a reasonable argument other than problems with the teacher for reassigning your child to another teacher. The issue here is not the reality of the primary (teacher) cause of the problem but what secondary causes will most effectively help you reach your original goal. Using secondary causes ultimately protects your child, diminishes the probability of friction, and provides an acceptable or excellent educational program.

Form F on page 205 in Chapter 8 will assist you with

objectivity when observing your child in a classroom situation. This form, unlike several of the others in Chapter 8, may be used during a conference with the teacher and/or administration. You may be surprised to discover that the teacher is not the primary cause of your child's difficulties after all.

▶ **Skill # 6: Enlist the present teacher as a friendly ally in requesting reassignment.**

This skill is one of the most difficult to master and utilize. It is not recommended as a first attempt for reassignment unless a parent is highly skilled in human relations and listening techniques, but if you can do it, it will be well worth the effort. Teachers are more cooperative when they are made to feel part of a "team effort" and included in the suggestion to change classrooms. If the idea for a new class assignment originates with the teacher, the likelihood of successfully achieving the goals is decidedly increased.

SUGGESTIONS:

1. Schedule an appointment for a one-to-one conference.

2. Establish rapport.

3. Use the (teacher) face-saving methods explained in Chapter 3.

4. Use the conference skills listed in Chapter 3.

5. Identify objective environmental elements which have led you to request a new classroom assignment. (These elements should not be a reflection upon the teacher's ability if you are seeking the teacher's support for the change.)

6. Seek appropriate and genuine means of expressing approval of the current teacher and the school.

7. Carefully consider the objections the teacher may have to your request. Be prepared with reasonable, logical responses. Practicing in advance of the conference may give you an advantage if you address the potential objections before the teacher brings them up in conversation.

Give yourself an "A+" in conference skills if you and a co-operative teacher make a joint request to the administration for reassignment!

After utilizing the skills in this chapter and other skills that you may discover as you work with your unique situation, it is still possible that you may not succeed in getting your child reassigned. It may become necessary to redefine your original goals. You might decide that it is impossible to provide for a smooth classroom transition without conflict. If this goal is rejected, it is probable that you will also have to reject the third goal: to continue to ensure positive school relationships for your child.

While I have emphasized that conflict is not desirable and will produce negative feelings among school personnel, it is conceivable that an extreme situation may, indeed, necessitate legal counsel. If, as a last resort, you must take legal action, then do so. Do not make the empty threat, "I'll sue." Administrators and teachers are becoming anesthetized to these kinds of threats. Many frustrated parents verbally attack and threaten, but few take quiet, deliberate action. The hostility of verbal attacks and threats has no positive, healing function.

Even legal action should be taken in a problem-solving mode. The key objective is to intelligently manage the situation and achieve your redefined goal(s). Hostility diminishes the satisfactory achievement of goals and, thus, has no place in effective EP-A/R activity. *Only goal-directed action is desirable!*

SUMMARY

REASSIGNMENT GOAL #1: TO HAVE AN ACCEPTABLE TEACHER ASSIGNED TO YOUR CHILD WITHOUT ALIENATING SCHOOL PERSONNEL.

REASSIGNMENT GOAL # 2: TO PROVIDE FOR A SMOOTH CLASSROOM TRANSITION WITHOUT CONFLICT.

REASSIGNMENT GOAL # 3: TO CONTINUE TO ENSURE POSITIVE SCHOOL RELATIONSHIPS FOR YOUR CHILD.

Reassignment Secrets

Secret # 1: School administrators are usually reluctant to move a child from an unacceptable teacher's classroom to another classroom.

Secret # 2: Children are reassigned during the school year to other teachers and programs.

Skills for Reassignment

Skill # 1: If appropriate, obtain a letter from your family physician suggesting the consideration of reassignment. This may be the least conflict-producing method for reassignment.

Skill # 2: Write constructive, objective concerns about the instructional program provided by the current teacher(s). Use Form A (page 185) and Form D (page 199) for assistance.

Skill # 3: Speak in terms of "alternative strategies" when you discuss classroom reassignment with administrators.

Skill # 4: Be prepared to address several questions which the administration or teacher(s) might ask.

Skill # 5: Creatively identify existing classroom environmental elements which could be the likely causes of your child's difficulties. Use Form F (page 205) for assistance.

Skill # 6: Enlist the present teacher as a friendly ally in requesting reassignment.

MOVING FORWARD . . .

We have discussed the importance of initial contact with the school, how to make conferences meaningful and productive, and how to have your child assigned to an acceptable classroom. We turn now to a discussion about positive visibility. What is it? How important is it to your child? How can it contribute to your role as an EP-A/R? How can volunteering services to the school affect positive visibility and your child? The next chapter addresses these questions, provides trust-building skills to improve parent volunteer–teacher relationships, and shares more secrets about the invisible school system.

5
Volunteering at School: Visibility at Its Best

You may recall that in previous chapters, I emphasized that *a visible parent can prevent a series of misfortunes* that occasionally befall children who are unrepresented or inadequately represented. This chapter explains why you need to find some time, however limited, for the school if at all possible, and how that time can best serve the needs of your child and others. It adds to the information and skills you have considered thus far concerning visibility in general. *Volunteering is discussed as a direct strategy of "Planned Positive Visibility."*

I want to emphasize at the outset, however, that in no way do I wish to suggest that you are doing your child a disservice if you do not volunteer to help the school. Many parents must work full-time and have a multitude of other equally pressing responsibilities. Others would feel uncomfortable working as a volunteer. My intent in this chapter is simply to identify one more potentially powerful position through which some can fulfill EP-A/R responsibilities.

WHY IS VISIBILITY IMPORTANT TO THE EP-A/R?

A substitute teacher had a difficult time with Sandra, a fifth grade girl, who was rude and disruptive. When the regular teacher, Ms. X, returned, she reprimanded Sandra in front of the class and demanded that Sandra apologize for her misbehavior to her and to the class. Sandra refused. As punishment for her rebellious attitude, Ms. X forced her to stand at the front of the room facing the class until she agreed to apologize. Class activities continued as Sandra stood. She was not permitted to do assignments or to speak. Two days elapsed in which this ten-year-old child spent approximately ten hours standing, staring at the class.

I suppose this would have continued until Ms. X had broken Sandra's will, had the administrator not intervened and put an end to the abuse and the ridiculous power struggle. The first day that he noticed Sandra in front of the room, he thought she probably was reading, reciting, or reporting to the class. At the end of the following day he saw her in front of the room again. This time he asked Ms. X about Sandra's assignment. She explained the details of the misconduct and punishment. He immediately removed Sandra from the classroom, and they had a heart-to-heart talk. She cried, saying that she hated her teacher and school. She had not told her parents of her suffering or misbehavior because she feared further punishment. Sandra didn't know how to get herself out of her predicament except to use the only option the teacher had offered, to apologize to the class, but her hatred for the teacher and determined sense of injustice were so strong that, I'm certain, she would have stood there several more days.

Ms. X, a woman who revelled in her power over others (teachers, children, parents, and administrators), was seething in anger at the administrator for undermining her authority.

Nevertheless, the idiotic punitive measure was aborted, and Sandra resumed her usual school activities. Sandra agreed that she owed the teacher an apology, but a private one between the two of them, not a public humiliation. Her fifth grade year continued to be emotionally upsetting for her.

After reading the previous chapters in this book, I'm certain that you appreciate the subtle psychological tortures that were inflicted for the remainder of the school year. Had one of Sandra's parents been "visible," this would probably not have happened. I have never, I repeat never, known of a child who was punished irresponsibly or harshly when a parent was visible in positive ways.

▷ **Secret #1: When teachers and administrators "slip" and behave in a less than professional manner, these slips are far less likely to involve children whose parents are positively visible at school and more likely to involve those children whose parents are extremely negative or who are totally uninvolved.** Even responsible, sensitive teachers have bad days just as loving parents occasionally overreact to a child's misbehavior or make errors in judgment.

There is a legend that someone once complimented Julius Caesar about the magnificently stable institution of Roman Law. Caesar is supposed to have wryly commented that "The Roman Law is truly a wonderful instrument for government. It works best, however, when the legions are in town." This means, of course, that behavior is controlled by consequences. The behavior of teachers is no exception. Your presence positively perceived has incredible power as it affects the teachers' behavior. It also affords you access to the invisible system.

▷ **Secret #2: When you are positively perceived and involved, professionals may share glimpses of the invisible system which they would not otherwise discuss with you.**

As caring, decent people (as most school people are) come to know and like you, your visibility will increasingly cause them one of the common paradoxical problems of a sophisticated society: a collision between their professional ethics (agreed-upon standards of behavior related to the management of a profession) and their personal morals (their "gut-level" feelings related to right and wrong). Attorneys experience this conflict when they have to offer their best defense for a client who they know is guilty of a heinous crime. Some physicians anguish when the law and the ethics of their profession demand that they fight for the life of a patient whose brain is no longer sending any electrical signals. Professional educators experience similar conflicts.

I know a teacher who believed that the entire group of teachers in the subsequent grade level were inept to perform their jobs. Out of compassion for a child who was especially gifted and whose mother was a room mother, the teacher violated the boundaries of professional ethics and told the mother that it would be wiser to withdraw her son from the school than to allow him to vegetate in any one of those teacher's classes the following school year. The mother took the teacher's advice and enrolled the child in another school for one year. The long-range benefits to the child were immeasurable.

I am neither supporting nor criticizing the teacher's action, only using it to illustrate the point.

This is the dilemma which your positive presence may create for the genuinely "good" people who work in public education. When they know and like you, they will feel conscious or subconscious pressure to subtly or directly provide you with information you need to make wise EP-A/R decisions.

You receive another bonus from the invisible system when your positively perceived presence causes a "smoother" to feel friendly to you and, thus, to your family. "Smoothers" are those who "know the ropes" of organizations, who have the knowledge and experience to smooth the bumpy roads of institutional politics and red tape. Though their jobs may have unimposing titles such as "secretary," or "aide," or "clerk," when smoothers take you under their wings, obstacles in the path of your EP-A/R success begin to tumble.

The concrete advantages to be gained for your child are obvious and lead us logically to our EP-A/R goal for this chapter.

GOAL: TO PLAN A REASONABLE STRATEGY OF POSITIVE VISIBILITY.

To achieve this goal, let's begin by exploring two broad categories of strategic options for positively perceived visibility: "Direct-Connects," and "Fast 'N' Easies." "Direct-Connects" are ways of being visible by giving specifically allocated time for school endeavors. "Fast 'N' Easies" are ways of being visible through casual encounters. They require little or no structured additional time out of your usual daily routine. That's what makes these visibility options "Fast 'N' Easy."

DIRECT-CONNECTS

1. Conferencing
   • Initiated by parents as a preventive measure
   • Necessitated by child's school experiences
   • Calls about child's progress (as a direct result of the conference)
   • Follow-up thank-you notes
2. Volunteering
   • Help at school on a regularly scheduled basis
   • Participate in volunteer training programs
   • Help to recruit other volunteers
   • Make instructional materials at home
   • Sharing skill, trade, or business expertise

3. Joining and Becoming Active in Parent-Teacher Associations—School or District Level or Both
4. Becoming a Homeroom Parent
   • Help with planned parties (help supervise, bring or send treats)
   • Help with class or individual projects
   • Assist with field trips
5. Visiting and Observing Your Child
   • Visit the classroom during prime instructional time (PIT) within the first few weeks of school

"FAST 'N' EASIES"

"Fast 'N' Easy" visibility options are limited only by your imagination. Below are a few ideas:

1. Share materials from your business.
2. Provide financial support to acquire needed equipment or new books for the library.
3. Donate plants, paintings, carpet, paint to make offices or the teachers' lounge more attractive or comfortable.
4. Surprise a team of teachers or the office staff with baked goods, fresh fruit, vegetables, hand-made articles, or any gesture of thoughtfulness to express appreciation. Hint: To these surprises, attach cards signed by you *and your child.* Perhaps, your child could present the gift.
5. Send regular notes expressing interest and support to your child's teacher, principal, and others who contribute to your child's daily welfare (e.g., music, art, library teachers, guidance counselors, lunchroom manager). Form G in Chapter 8 may help you learn of ideal times to recognize these special people.
6. Compliment specific individuals when you casually encounter them at school. Example: When you take or pick up your child, learn the names of those you will meet on a regular basis; knowing their names is a compliment. Offer sincere compliments about the school program: field trips, plays, decor, facility, children's art and music program, etc.

7. Give special recognition to those teachers who "moonlight," who attend your church, or who are members of organizations to which you also belong. Example: Make a button or sign that says, "An outstanding teacher works here . . . belongs to our group . . . helps at our church. . . ."

"Fast 'N' Easies" are intended to communicate an attitude of gratitude and support, not one of currying favor. Your strategy of visibility needs to be naturally genuine, like the father's in the following story: An outstanding first grade teacher had in her class a child whose father worked for a nursery. To express his appreciation, throughout the entire year he provided beautiful plants for her room. All of the second grade teachers knew the family name and had at one time or another commented that they hoped to have that child in their class the next school year. They had a positive image of the father and his child before meeting them. What a pleasant second grade beginning for his child to be wanted by all of the teachers!

Your strategy for Planned Positive Visibility will probably include a combination of options in each of the two categories. After realistically evaluating your resources of time, personality, talents, and finances, you're ready to implement the best visibility plan for you and your family. Planning + Your Positive Visibility = Better Education for Your Child.

VOLUNTEERING: A MODEL STRATEGY

Among all the options, volunteering is the most effective strategy for positive visibility. When I was twenty-six, I taught a fourth and fifth grade combination class in a school populated primarily with children from lower socio-economic families. Most of my twenty-seven students were functioning below grade level in reading and math, while a few were well above grade level. Their needs ranged from kindergarten reading readiness skills to those of sixth grade. There was no doubt in my mind that I could teach them best working with them one-to-one and in small groups. But, of course, as is often the case in such situations, in their earlier school experiences many of these children had also defined themselves as behavior problems, adding yet another dimension to the challenge of classroom management. I found myself fantasizing about how much farther they could progress if there was another adult to assist them with assigned tasks and test individual achievement of identified skills. If only I had four hands, two heads, and could be in several places at once, I could do so much more for them.

Then, along came Linda! She was an answer to my students' needs and my dreams. She spoke two languages, had a degree in education, and had taught elementary school in Holland. She said that she enjoyed working with children and felt that she had a lot to share. She asked relevant questions relating to the tasks I outlined for the students. Our planning time together always focused on the instructional program for the children. She tested students, assisted them with assignments, and taught them many things about other cultures. She respected cultural differences and never caused a child to feel unacceptable.

When we had lunch together or a few extra minutes after school, we talked about our families and other personal matters. She chose these times to specifically compliment me about the students' progress, my instructional methods, and overall program. She kindly and gently spoke of job frustrations she thought that I might experience. She helped "recharge my battery."

In addition to her emotional support and caring, she brought me occasional gifts just to say she enjoyed working with me. I found it easy and natural to reciprocate.

Several of my students jumped ahead two and three grade levels as evidenced by standardized test results. These students' educational experiences were dramatically improved because of dear, dear, Linda. They and I are forever in her debt. Probably they have long forgotten her; I never will.

Linda performed a very special kind of magic for my students and me and deeply enriched her own life, but she was unusually fortunate to have large portions of time to spend as she chose. In general, the *amount* of time spent positively visible is not nearly as important as the *quality* of that time. Many mistakenly believe that volunteer work requires hours upon precious hours spent in the school. The pleasant truth for all of us hardworking parents is that any service, even a single hour, may be interpreted as volunteer work and affords opportunities for the needed visibility.

Teacher Resistance to Volunteers

Perhaps you are presently giving time to your child's school or have attempted in the past to become actively involved, but your experiences have taught you that the teachers and administrators don't want you there, that they say "We want volunteers" out of one side of their mouths and out of the other gossip about how much trouble it is to have parents around.

As more demands are placed upon teachers, they are becoming better educated about classroom-volunteer program management. They are increasingly attuned to the invaluable assistance available from the community. Yet, even with this new-found awareness, many teachers are ambivalent about volunteer/parent help. Teachers have the potential, as do we all, to be a difficult, cantankerous lot. Some want the help they want when they want it without performing the related necessary tasks of recruiting, planning, and nurturing the teacher-volunteer relationship. They expect the volunteer to do as told without asking questions, seeking to understand, or wanting to be part of the overall program. The attitude communicated is, "Just come to my classroom totally selflessly and serve me and the children." They want the help, but do not want to pay any price for the services.

As a former coordinator of school-level volunteer programs, I know that volunteering is beneficial to volunteers, teachers, and children. Why is it then that occasionally these relationships sour, leaving the bitter aftertaste of disappointment, defeat, and rejection? Why do some teachers resist the presence of parent volunteers? The following secrets will answer these questions by highlighting attitudes that inhibit effective volunteer-teacher relationships.

▷ **Secret #3: Some teachers are intimidated by the presence of a parent volunteer because of personal insecurities and/or because they lack the training necessary to effectively coordinate volunteer services.**

Some are threatened by the presence of parents in their classrooms. Many competent teachers, as well as those whose abilities are marginal or nonexistent, suffer from anxiety over being judged, analyzed, and talked about. This anxiety is accentuated if that teacher lacks training for the use of classroom volunteers. He may want and need you but not know how to effectively use your time, and therefore, avoid having to deal with you at all.

It is, however, an error to assume that a teacher must be unqualified if he chooses not to have a volunteer parent in the classroom. All of us who have experienced anxieties and insecurities can empathize with capable teachers who cause themselves unnecessary anguish. Some are simply not prepared to deal with the eager parent on their doorstep.

▷ **Secret #4: The "familiar" can become so comfortable that a teacher may resist even advantageous change.**

Volunteering is certainly not a revolutionary new idea, but for some teachers who have never had a volunteer in their classrooms, it represents a threatening change. These teachers prefer status quo to constructive growth in spite of the current societal changes that pressure them to move toward healthy classroom reconstruction. They suspect every innovation, every change in schedule, every opportunity for improvement. Their Language Masters, Tutorettes, listening centers, and tape recorders—all expensive invaluable equipment for providing an individualized instructional program—collect dust in a closet. While others could be putting this equipment to good use, these teachers hoard what is theirs, carefully checking the locks on the storage closets before going home each afternoon. They could dust off the equipment, plan instructional objectives, and train volunteers to help students use the equipment. Ah, there's the rub! This would disturb the status quo—their daily routine—and make demands upon them. Will they next add computers to their dust collection?

▷ **Secret #5: When teachers believe that parent volunteers are difficult, nosy, or bothersome, they consciously work to keep them out of their classrooms.**

The key word is *believe*. You may be easy-going and amiable, but the teacher may believe otherwise about volunteers in general. I consistently shared with other teachers my good fortune and delight in finding Linda. Despite her obvious contributions to the students' overall progress, however, many of the other teachers' comments were primarily expressions of fear, discomfort, and distrust, such as: "Why don't you put her in the hall with a child?" "Doesn't it take up too much of your time showing her what needs to be done?" "Doesn't she get in your way?" "Doesn't she waste your time talking about things that have nothing to do with your work?" "Are you worried that she'll talk about you?" Or they made excuses for not using volunteer help such as: "I would use a volunteer, but I just can't find the time to plan for one." "Volunteers always gossip about the things that happen in class." "It's just more trouble than it's worth."

These teachers' predisposition to fear change, their lack of understanding and training about the multiple advantages of volunteer help, and their personal anxieties prevented them from helping themselves and their students.

In addition to these barriers, some teachers prefer not to use volunteer services because of previously discouraging personal experiences or those of their colleagues. One of the main reasons that these teachers are not overjoyed at the prospect of volunteer help is that no matter how well intentioned some volunteers are, a few of them don't finish what they start. After a teacher has spent time and energy training a volunteer and adjusting the schedule, and has come to rely upon the welcomed assistance of another adult, it is disconcerting to have that person abruptly decide to withdraw the agreed-upon services. When this kind of event becomes school gossip, other teachers may be led to believe that using volunteer help is a waste of valuable professional time.

Considering what may at first glimpse appear to be insurmountable attitudinal resistance, you may wonder if peaceful coexistence is possible between professionals and volunteers. The answer is, decidedly, yes! Thank goodness for the thousands of Linda stories.

When I was appointed as the Primary Specialist for the largest elementary school in our district, I became the school's volunteer program coordinator, as well. In cooperation with many talented professionals at the school who already had an excellent volunteer program in progress, I expanded it, and we had over sixty-five active, productive volunteers. This program was recognized by the County and the State for its excellence. The teachers, administrators, and office staff encouraged and supported the volunteers, nurturing a mutually rewarding relationship; and together, they, not I, made the program work for the children. These kinds of programs are working effectively throughout our nation because teachers and volunteers can work well together for the good of our children.

Steps to Take If You Plan to Volunteer

Your first step is to analyze your motives for volunteering. When logical people consider any new course of action, they ask themselves, "What are the advantages and disadvantages?" Teachers also entertain this question when volunteers offer help. If the teacher believes that the disadvantages outweigh the advantages or perceives a threat, she will tend to resist volunteer aid. The success of the volunteer-teacher relationship depends upon the development of mutual trust. Our motives for volunteering affect that level of trust because people send subliminal signals that expose their "real" attitudes. These attitudes reflect our primary and secondary motives for volunteering. Only those motives perceived as "acceptable" to the teacher and school staff can predictably build mutual trust. There are basically two "acceptable" primary motives for volunteering:

• To maximize your ability to serve your child through positive school visibility;
• To broaden and improve the services the school provides for all children.

Having recruited and trained volunteers, I have heard many highly acceptable secondary motives for choosing to help. Some people like the beauty and openness of children and enjoy being around them. Some would like to demonstrate their abilities so that when positions open, they have an inside track. Some who have been out of the job market foresee the future need for a letter of reference and may wish the opportunity to make a positive impression upon the school administration. Some want to experience the teaching process firsthand before deciding to choose education as a career. Many retired teachers who enjoy teaching, volunteer in order to stay vigorous by using their skills and by offering a service that they know is genuinely valuable and needed. Finally, there are those who are lonely and who take steps to assuage their loneliness in a positive and healthy manner; they seek companionship and affection by being willing to earn it. They help children grow and learn. There are, then, numerous worthwhile, legitimate, nonthreatening motives beyond pure altruism for volunteering.

The second step is to commit yourself to a plan for volunteer visibility. Decide to give a definite portion of time to the school.

Third, bravely contact the school and start the ball rolling. Make an appointment with the individual who coordinates the school's volunteer program or with your child's teacher. Ask about needs of the children, the teachers, and the school. Discuss your interests and abilities and the amount of time you feel comfortable giving. The coordinator should make efforts to match your interests to school needs.

The final step is an important one: to develop trust-building skills. After defining acceptable motivation, trust-building becomes a matter of employing adequately developed interpersonal skills to build and maintain peaceful, productive volunteer-teacher relationships.

INTERPERSONAL TRUST-BUILDING SKILLS

▶ **Skill # 1: Make commitments you can keep.**

First-time volunteers are often carried away with momentary enthusiasm that causes them to overcommit themselves. I recommend that you start volunteering by giving just a few limited hours of your time. Then, if the experience is unsatisfactory, you can still "tough it out" for the duration of your promise to help. Those who begin slowly usually enjoy themselves, are a tremendous bonus to the school, and are long-time dependable volunteers.

The purpose of positive visibility will be better served when you offer as little as two hours a month to grade papers in your home and faithfully fulfill your pledge, than when you promise to give five hours a week and don't live up to that promise.

▶ **Skill #2: Be punctual.**

Punctuality shows respect for the educational process and for the people you are affecting when you arrive on time prepared to help.

▶ **Skill #3: Be thorough and conscientious.**

A job half done is better not attempted in the first place. Agree to do only those things you know you will be able to do conscientiously and thoroughly.

▶ **Skill #4: Be dependably pleasant and positive.**

The teacher should be able to expect you to be in a pleasant and positive mood each time you assist because of the many previous "pleasant" encounters you have had.

▶ **Skill #5: Deal with problems rationally rather than emotionally.**

Discuss issues of concern rather than complaining about them. Seek rational alternative solutions to problems rather than "exploding."

▶ **Skill #6: Be part of the solution, not part of the problem.**

The following list of do's and don'ts clarifies how volunteers may be part of solutions rather than creators of or participants in problems:

Do's	Don'ts
Do speak clearly, concisely, and directly.	Don't waste the teacher's valuable time discussing pointless details.
Do be flexible; adapt cheerfully to sudden changes in plans. Your attitude helps the teacher adjust more effortlessly to unexpected change. Be prepared for your routine to change occasionally; it will!	Don't be rigid! Children and schedules may necessitate unexpected changes. You can cope!

Do's	Don'ts
Do talk with the teacher at appropriate times (e.g. appointments, planning sessions, perhaps during the children's play period).	Don't corner the teacher during instructional times when the students need his undivided attention.
Do ask questions relevant to your tasks.	Don't pry about issues that are irrelevant to your relationship with the school and about which you could do nothing constructive.
Do share in the joy of children's achievements. Be confidential about all children's and teachers' problems you may encounter. Share positive experiences about working with the school family.	Don't gossip with teachers or other parents about children's problems at school. Don't gossip about the school family.
Do dress appropriately for the day's events.	Don't overdress (e.g., if you're going to fingerpaint with children). Don't underdress (e.g., if you're helping on a field trip to a museum).
Do have fun doing whatever you select. There are multiple ways to help. Tell the volunteer coordinator, teacher, or principal the kinds of things you enjoy, and let her match your interests and needs to that of the school's interests and needs.	Don't allow yourself to be assigned to something that is not suited to your ability or inclination. You and the school are better served when you're doing something suited to your abilities and tastes.

▶ **Skill #7: Find productive ways to be of "real" service.**
There are so many ways to be of service that an entire
chapter could be dedicated to that alone. Below are a few
suggestions to start creative thoughts flowing:

• Show an interest in the teachers' efforts to meet the
complex demands of their jobs.
• Assist with paperwork: grading, recording, reports.
• Share a special talent, craft, skill, or experience with students.
• Relieve teachers of clerical tasks such as filing and storage of materials.
• Help staff other than teachers (e.g., the office staff, the li-
brarian, the nurse).
• Accept partial or full responsibility for school newspa-
pers, photography for bulletin board projects, artistic displays, or informational displays.
• Help with fund-raising projects for an improved school
environment and curriculum (e.g., new equipment and sup-
plies).

▶ **Skill #8: Contract for less than you are planning to
give or give more than you contract for.**
Whether it is just or not, after a time people come to feel
that we ought to do what we agreed to do, even when our efforts are gratis. It is delightful to know those who, when it is
appropriate, regularly do more than is expected. Skill #1
suggested that volunteers limit their commitments to be sure
that they can keep them, but there is another reason for limit-
ing your original commitment; it provides you with the flexibility to do those little extras, extras that are unexpected and
welcomed surprises.

▶ **Skill #9: Be a good listener.**
People who regularly interrupt, who always have a better
story, or who seem to be waiting for the one speaking to
breathe so that they can begin to talk, communicate that they

are discounting the value of the other person's ideas. Listening attentively and making appropriate responses communicates respect and a genuine appreciation for another.

▶ **Skill # 10: Be patient.**
We don't receive the trust of others by telling them that we are trustworthy. We need to be patient and allow time for that truth to establish itself. Trust-building is, itself, an interpersonal skill. Not all nuts can be cracked nor all barriers removed. Some teachers will never be amenable to volunteer help; some anxieties are too deep; some wounds will not heal. But, trust-building efforts will improve nearly all human relationships. BONUS: *They will improve the life of the one making the effort.*

A FINAL WORD ABOUT VOLUNTEERING

Teachers who want volunteers will also make efforts to build trust. Listed here are a few things teachers should and should not do if they want to build your confidence in them:

Shoulds	*Should Nots*
They should accept full responsibility for the class at all times.	They shouldn't leave you alone in charge of a class. Certificated personnel are legally responsible for the total physical, academic, and social welfare of all their students.
They should have reasonable expectations.	They shouldn't expect too much, too soon, or too often.
They should explain all tasks clearly and thoroughly. They should encourage questions and strive to give responsible answers.	They should not give you unexplained assignments. Everyone, including teachers, needs to understand the purpose and value of work.

Shoulds	Should Nots
They should compliment you in front of children and adults. They should be specific about the kind of help that is appreciated.	They should not publicly criticize you or gossip about you to other parents, volunteers, the school family, or in the presence of children.
They should treat you as part of a team, because you are! You have needs too!	They shouldn't treat you as an outsider who is there only to gratify their needs. They should not ignore the "plus" you are to the school team.
They should nurture relationships that benefit the children. They should terminate parent-volunteer/school relationships that are detrimental to students.	They should not, as professionals, continue relationships that minimize their classroom effectiveness.

SUMMARY

GOAL: TO PLAN A REASONABLE STRATEGY OF POSITIVE VISIBILITY.

Secrets About the Power of Visibility

Secret # 1: When teachers and administrators "slip" and behave in a less than professional manner, these "slips" are far less likely to involve children whose parents are positively visible at school and more likely to involve those children whose parents are extremely negative or who are totally uninvolved.

Secret # 2: When you are positively perceived and involved, professionals may share glimpses of the invisible system which they would not otherwise discuss with you.

Secrets About Resistance to Volunteer Parents

Secret #3: Some teachers are intimidated by the presence of a parent volunteer because of personal insecurities and/or because they lack the training necessary to effectively coordinate volunteer services.

Secret #4: The "familiar" can become so comfortable that a teacher may resist even advantageous change.

Secret #5: When teachers believe parent volunteers to be difficult, nosy, or bothersome, they consciously work to keep them out of their classrooms.

Interpersonal Trust-Building Skills

Skill #1: Make commitments you can keep.

Skill #2: Be punctual.

Skill #3: Be thorough and conscientious.

Skill #4: Be dependably pleasant and positive.

Skill #5: Deal with problems rationally rather than emotionally.

Skill #6: Be part of the solution, not part of the problem.

Skill #7: Find productive ways to be of "real" service.

Skill #8: Contract for less than you are planning to give or give more than you contract for.

Skill #9: Be a good listener.

Skill #10: Be patient.

REMEMBER: Volunteering is not right for every EP-A/R, but positive visibility is! Your presence positively perceived by school personnel may be the single greatest advantage you can provide for your child as an EP-A/R. Find the means of visibility that best suits you, and give it as a gift to your child.

MOVING FORWARD . . .

Millions of youngsters are involved in programs provided for children who have special educational needs beyond the mainstream curriculum designed to serve the majority. These programs often welcome volunteer assistance and may be an avenue you will want to investigate at your child's school. But, for now let's explore the complex world of special services for these exceptional children.

6

Programs for "Exceptional" Children and Programs for "Disadvantaged" Children: Can They Help Your Child?

WHAT PROGRAM IS THE RIGHT PROGRAM? WHICH DIRECTION IS THE RIGHT DIRECTION?

Once upon a time there was a brave, daring, and intelligent young woman, named Gretta, who lived in a village in which many of the children suffered from a malady affecting their ability to learn. It was said that there was a magic formula hidden in the words of the Acronyms which could heal the children and allow them to grow naturally. Gretta was asked by the people of her village to journey to the world of the Acronyms and learn their language. Now this was a language no one from her village had ever been able to understand. Some grasped a few words, here and there, but no one had discovered the secret sequence that would unleash the power of the magic. Gretta was awed by the importance of her mission.

It was said by the village wise men that the Acronyms were a strange people who could only be understood if one attended their colleges and earned their degrees, and even then some of the Acronym people couldn't understand one another. So the wise men tried to prepare Gretta for her journey. She was told to be a good listener, to take notes, and upon her return to report everything to the people of her village. She set off with grave determination. One day, not long after she had left, a guard in the highest tower spied her while she was yet afar off and jubilantly shouted down the news of her return. Her friends and neighbors rushed out to meet her, eager to hear of the magic cure. As they ran around the bend in the road and came face to face with Gretta, they halted abruptly, shaken by her appearance.

Head bowed, body bent, eyes glazed and confused, she confessed, "My dear people, I have failed you woefully. Even when the people are friendly and try to be helpful, it's difficult to travel in a land where one doesn't speak the language. When I entered the gates of Acronymia, I saw many streets pointing in diverse directions. Some roads looked straight and smooth. Others appeared to have turns and twists with rough terrain. Of course, I needed just the right path to reach their Temple where dwell their wise men who, I thought, would help me reach my goal of understanding the mysteries of their language and world. The streets had odd and unfamiliar names: SLD, EMH, TMH, PMH, SLH, IEP, VI, EH, HI, OT, and many more. I was confused and frightened because only one was the right path, and I couldn't be sure which it was. Fortunately, a delegation met me just inside the gate. They asked me to conference with them at something called an ECE conference at the conclusion of which they promised to help me choose the correct path to reach my goal. As we sat in the meeting, I listened very carefully. They all had difficult titles and different advice. The psychologist recommended EH; the guidance counselor, SLD; the speech therapist, SLH; the principal said not to bother because the wise men were too busy to help me with my goal even if I found the right path; the special reading teacher said only eight people could go down the ECIA road in one group—it was always full and had nothing to do with ECE programs anyway—so take SLD.

The longest path, one that would have taken all year, was suggested by the regular teacher, who said that the meeting was beginning to be annoying and taking entirely too much time.

"It was a mandatory part of their sacred tradition that at the conclusion of the meeting, one of their number must write something called an IEP that would explain exactly which was prescribed. Before writing it, the chosen one turned to me and asked which one I thought best. I was confused, but they seemed so in earnest and in need of an answer that I looked at all of the streets and randomly selected HI. It was the only word I recognized. 'Good idea,' they all exclaimed, and the chosen one happily wrote the IEP. But I didn't understand the directions on the IEP. I was embarrassed to tell them that I still didn't understand, for they all had seemed so pleased about the outcome of the ECE conference. I couldn't find my way to HI, and I feared to try any other unknown path. So I turned my back on the gates of Acronymia, defeated and frustrated.

"I don't blame them. They were good people. They urged me to try to learn their ways, assuring me that in time all mysteries would be revealed, but they didn't seem interested in trying to learn our ways. As they closed their gates, I thought I heard them laughing. They must be very happy people with one another. As a stranger in their land, they tried to teach me, to advise me, to direct me, but they didn't try to know me. Without learning their language, I was never comfortable with them. But their language was impossibly difficult, and all I really needed was their secret formula. It was their tradition that I had to successfully play a game with them in order to get it, but I couldn't learn the rules. And so I have come home where the children still struggle to learn. There would never be a reason for us to seek to communicate if it weren't for the children. If it just were not for the children. . . ."

Gretta knew the frustration that parents experience when

attempting to understand the Exceptional Child Programs, often known as "Special Student Services" or "Special Ed." Under this broad heading, there are many programs with imposing titles that are usually abbreviated by educators, for example, SLD (Specific Learning Disabilities), EH (Emotionally Handicapped). These abbreviations and program titles used in conferences invariably perplex parents and force them into the role of tolerated outsiders. No wonder they seem to shun the educator's village. The language of the Exceptional Child Education Programs is not intended to be secretive or to exclude parents. As in most professions, an "insider" functional language has simply evolved and is used automatically and often unconsciously around parents.

Exceptional Child Education (ECE) Programs are special education programs offered in the public schools for children who are identified as "handicapped" or "gifted" and whose exceptional educational needs could not be satisfied in the mainstream curriculum. These programs are supported and regulated by the federal government and the states. Guidelines and criteria differ among the districts and states and often from year to year within the same state.

It should not be surprising then that many parents are confused about these programs because many professional educators flounder in the quagmire of perpetual change in officially accepted program definitions, guidelines, and criteria for student participation. These changes are unavoidable. Federal and state relationships are in constant flux which affects the localities, and the localities' educational needs change as the communities' needs change (e.g., a sudden explosion in the immigrant or refugee population affects the educational needs of the community). These local changes force the state and federal governments to respond. And so it goes. The parents' camp will struggle to understand the educators' camp because even the educators jump about spasmodically in response to fluctuating needs of the community. End result: Parents and educators alike are confused about

Exceptional Child Program issues such as services, responsibilities, criteria for student eligibility, and program implementation. Further confusion arises because at the same time there exist federally supported and regulated remedial programs in the public schools intended to help educationally "disadvantaged" students. What is the distinction between ECE programs and these programs? Who belongs where?

This chapter cannot hope to fully clarify all these issues. It is not a textbook about the "exceptionalities" or learning problems. It will not address the various handicaps or giftedness. It is a cursory examination of a few school system secrets about Exceptional Child Education Programs and federal education programs for the disadvantaged. Knowledge of these secrets can help you overcome much of the anxiety you may feel about granting permission for your child to participate in a program about which you might know very little or nothing at all. EP-A/R goals and skills are also discussed so that you need not be a frustrated Gretta. Armed with this knowledge you can open the school gates, understand the language, and ensure that your child participates in only those programs that will be predictably supportive of her healthy development.

EXCEPTIONAL CHILD EDUCATION PROGRAMS (SPECIAL STUDENT SERVICES)

Let's begin by coming to appreciate what "exceptional" means as it applies to handicapped or disabled and gifted children served by public schools.

Who Are Exceptional Children?

"Of course," a parent proclaims, "my child is exceptional. She plays the flute beautifully." In common usage, "exceptional" leads us to envision one with outstanding ability or talent. Surprise! It isn't so in Acronymia. In Acronymia the term *exceptional* basically is applied to those children who deviate from the norm (average). The gifted and handicapped or disabled are all "exceptional" because they are those with abilities above or below or with some other deviation from the "average or normal child," *and* they require special educational program modification to meet their needs. If the child who played the flute well was not participating in any Exceptional Education Program, then she would not, administratively speaking, be "exceptional."

Samuel A. Kirk and James J. Gallegher, in their book *Educating Exceptional Children,* define the exceptional child as "the child who deviates from the average or normal child (1) in mental characteristics, (2) in sensory abilities, (3) in neuromotor or physical characteristics, (4) in social behavior, (5) in communication abilities, or (6) in multiple handicaps. Such deviation must be of such an extent that the child requires a modification of school practices, or special educational services, to develop to maximum capacity." Instead of memorizing all that, it's sufficient for an effective EP-A/R to develop an understanding that, administratively speaking, exceptional students are those designated by the school system as requiring special student services that are beyond the regular classroom curriculum.

Let's take a closer look at the two major exceptional children categories: the "handicapped" or "disabled" and the "gifted."

Who Is Handicapped or Disabled?

When you visit a school, you may see a child in a wheelchair. Is he "disabled" or "handicapped"? According to Exceptional Child Education criteria, it is very possible that he may be neither. If the child attends only the regular school classes and requires no curriculum change different from that of the "average" child, then in public school that child is not "disabled." In terms of ECE programs, a handicap or disability is a condition that adversely affects a student's ability to learn within the framework of the mainstream curriculum. The condition might be a specific learning disability (a disorder in one or more of the basic psychological processes involved in understanding or in using spoken or written language), or a visual, hearing, or motor handicap, mental retardation, or an emotional disturbance. To be identified "handicapped" or "disabled" in this sense, a student must be tested and evaluated by experts according to standards defined by the special education regulations of your state and by guidelines and criteria of the district in which you reside.

Below is an alphabetical listing of several titles of Exceptional Child Programs for the disabled or handicapped, but keep in mind that titles for ECE programs do vary from state to state. In this chapter, I will refer to the commonly used titles as listed here. If your child is being considered for any exceptional child program or "special student services," you'll want to request the current county and state definitions of categories of students that may be served by that program. College and city libraries will also have a wealth of information about exceptional children.

Exceptional Child Education (ECE) Program Titles	Commonly Referred To As:
1. Educable Mentally Handicapped or Educable Mentally Retarded	EMH EMR (same program)
2. Emotionally Handicapped or Emotionally Disturbed	EH ED (same program)
3. Gifted	Gifted
4. Hospital and Homebound Children	Homebound
5. Profoundly Mentally Handicapped or Profoundly Mentally Retarded	PMH PMR (same program)
6. Specific Learning Disabilities	SLD RESOURCE (part-time student participation)

Exceptional Child Education (ECE) Program Titles	Commonly Referred To As:
	SLD FULL-TIME student participation
7. Speech-, Language-, Hearing- Impaired	SLH RESOURCE (part-time student participation)
	SLH FULL-TIME student participation
8. Trainable Mentally Handicapped or Trainable Mentally Retarded	TMH⎫ (same program) TMR⎭
9. Visually Impaired	VI RESOURCE (part-time student participation)
	VI FULL-TIME student participation
10. Visually Handicapped	VH

There are numerous associations and organizations concerned with the interests of exceptional children. For your convenience, listed below are a few of those organizations, their addresses, and phone numbers.

Association for Children and Adults with Learning
Disabilities
4156 Library Rd.
Pittsburgh, PA 15234
(412) 341-1515

Association For Children with Retarded
Mental Development
817 Broadway
New York, NY 10003
(212) 475-7200

American Speech-Language-Hearing Association
10801 Rockville Pike
Rockville, MD 20852
(301) 897-5700

American Association on Mental Deficiency
1719 Kalorama Rd., N.W.
Washington, D.C. 20009
(202) 387-1968

National Association for Gifted Children
2070 County Rd. H.
St. Paul, MN 55112
(612) 784-3475

If you wish more information about any of the multitude of Exceptional Child Programs, your city library should be able to help you find the appropriate organization and its address. The directors, coordinators, and counselors of Special Student Services in your school district may also guide you toward helpful associations.

An Important Law for the Handicapped

The 1975 Federal Law entitled "The Education for All Handicapped Children Act," Public Law 94-142, calls for the "least restrictive placement alternative" and for a written Individual Education Plan (IEP) for all children designated "disabled." The "least restrictive environment" is referred to by educators as the process of "mainstreaming," which simply means that the plan for accommodating children's special needs should restrict them as little as possible from involvement in the mainstream of student life.

In the last decade there has been a pervasive push to teach handicapped children with their "normal" peers, providing for peer group interaction in the least restrictive educational environment. The assumption is that children will profit from encountering one another's unique abilities and disabilities. Is that true? We will have to wait until more evidence is available. Mainstreaming will work for some children, in some communities, at some ages, and will not work for others. If your child is identified handicapped or disabled, it's important for you to understand PL 94-142 and its implications as they affect your child's daily school schedule and curriculum.

Who Are the Gifted Children?

This question is often answered by stating the IQ of a child. For example, "My child is gifted. Her IQ is 130." This naive statement demonstrates two common misconceptions among parents: (1) that there is a universally accepted numerical standard called "IQ" (intelligence quotient) for determining giftedness, and (2) that the nature of giftedness is identified by IQ information alone.

Let's quickly clarify these misunderstandings. First, state and district definitions of gifted children change as the criteria for acceptance into the gifted programs change. For example, a state might define "gifted" as an IQ of 130 or better during one school year and change the criterion to an IQ of 135 or above the subsequent school year. Under these circumstances, a child with an IQ of 130 could be "gifted" one year and not the next.

The gifted program criteria for acceptance also vary among states. For example, you might live in a state that uses an IQ of 130 or better to identify gifted children. If you move to another state that uses an IQ of 140 or better to award that distinction, your "gifted" child would no longer be "gifted."

This leads us to our second misconception: that giftedness is identified solely by obtaining a high IQ score. While it is generally accepted that the common denominator for gifted children is intellectual superiority, that superiority may manifest itself in several ways that are "observable," but may not be easily "testable," such as leadership ability and accelerated academic achievement. Many other observable qualities may clearly demonstrate praiseworthy and outstanding ability such as unusual performance in art or music, but these qualities may not be listed as "observable traits" on a state's or district's question-and-answer forms for identifying the "gifted."

There are yet other problems with reference to the comment, "My child has a 130 IQ." First, studies give much evidence that IQ changes and can be increased with education and improved environmental factors. It doesn't necessarily denote "native intellectual potential" as many assume. An IQ is not fixed. Second, IQ scores may vary as much as ten points on either side of an obtained test score. For example, a child scoring a 100 IQ today could score 110 or 90 next year. Intelligence is not a concrete inanimate object that can be pinned down like a flower to a lapel for all to see. Instead of thinking that a child has an IQ of 130, it would be more correct to think of the child as having an IQ of 120 to 140.

What does all of this mean about your gifted child? If your child is evaluated for the gifted program and does not qualify, does this mean that your child is not "gifted"? Yes, because *gifted* is a professional and legal term setting the boundaries for funding programs and *selectively* identifying observable and testable criteria. It makes no universally understood statement about the ability of a child. Your child may be profoundly talented as observed by everyone she comes into contact with, including her teachers, but her IQ, which is "testable," may rank "gifted" in Florida but not in Wyoming, and her talent may be rated as "observably gifted" in Arizona but not in Oregon.

ECE Placement Procedures: It Helps to Understand How a Child Qualifies for These Programs

The ECE referral and evaluation procedures may vary from state to state and even between the districts within each state. To complicate the matter further, different ECE programs require different steps to be taken by those making the referral and by those evaluating. Therefore, it is impossible to identify the exact steps indicated for every ECE program nationwide. However, it is probably helpful to outline the basic requirements involved in the placement process before discussing goals, secrets, and skills that will relate to them. Summarized here in the broadest possible terms are the basic steps used to identify, refer, evaluate, and finally to place a child in an ECE program.

1. *Identification:* Someone recognizes that a child has a mental, emotional, or physical problem or perhaps a combination of these. That recognition could be by a parent, a teacher, an administrator, a school nurse, or any staff member. Children's problems are often identified during routine health and educational screenings when they enter school and throughout their school career.

2. *Referral:* This is a written document that formally states what has been identified as the reasons for requesting further screening and/or evaluation. It is perfectly acceptable at this point in the referral and evaluation process if the identification of the problem is vague. One of the purposes of a thorough evaluation is to attempt to specifically identify the problem(s).

3. *Consent for Evaluation:* The parents' permission is obtained for evaluative services. Parents will also be given a written statement pertaining to their rights regarding these services. Informed consent is necessary.

4. *Testing:* Evaluation is a multidisciplinary approach. Several professionals (among them school psychologists) are usually involved and many different tests administered. This prevents a child's placement in a program on the basis of the results of one test and one evaluator. This is an important safeguard. Even in large school districts school psychologists

usually service several schools. Therefore, after parents have given permission for testing, there may be a waiting period before the testing is actually completed. This period of time is not necessarily a matter of first come first served because some children's identified problems represent an immediate crisis. For instance, their behavior might constitute a danger to themselves and others. Judgments must be made concerning which cases receive priority for testing.

5. *Interpretation of Test Results:* A conference is held to discuss whether or not a child qualifies, according to the test results, for placement in one or more of the ECE programs. For example, a child could be in the speech and language program and in the gifted program.

   a. At this conference, often referred to as a staffing, or a Child Study Team Conference, or an ECE Conference, the "least restrictive environment" for the child is discussed. This means that the child is supposed to be scheduled for as much of the mainstream curriculum as is possible and still meet his exceptional needs.

   b. The Individual Educational Program (IEP) is also discussed. An IEP is developed for every child who participates in an ECE program. This is required under Public Law 94-142. In most cases it will be written by the ECE teacher(s) who will instruct the child if the child obtains placement. Other specialists, such as the speech and hearing teacher or the guidance counselor may have input, and parents are invited to participate in the planning process. A few important aspects of the IEP are: instructional objectives and goals written specifically to meet the needs of the child; the amount of time that the child will spend in the ECE program(s) and in the core curriculum provided in the child's regular classroom; and the date the IEP is written because future evaluation is based upon that date.

   c. Appropriate signatures are obtained before the child

can participate in the program. You will receive another copy of your rights and a copy of signed documents which usually have the signatures of all those in attendance. This must include the parent's signature or the child cannot participate. There are rare exceptions to this of course. And I emphasize rare. In the event that parents will not approve a program placement for their child that a school board deems essential to the child's welfare, that school board may take legal measures.

6. *Child Participation in Program(s)*: Participation should begin promptly after the conference and instruction will be based upon the IEP.

7. *IEP Annual Review:* Every year from the date of the original IEP a new program is developed for the forthcoming year. Parents are asked to be part of the planning process.

8. *Tri-Annual Re-evaluation:* Every three years it is legally stipulated that ECE children receive another complete evaluation to determine whether or not the current placement is still appropriate. This evaluation may occur more frequently upon the parent's request or upon the request of one of the professionals involved with the child.

Please keep in mind that though these last paragraphs may have read much like an article in an educational journal, it is essential to present this information for better understanding of the secrets and skills presented in this chapter. It is also important to note that at any point along the way during this process a parent may intervene and prevent further evaluation. However, test results may add to your decisions regarding the best educational program for your child, and should you decide not to permit program placement, that choice is always open to you. Of course, throughout the evaluation process those evaluating your child may determine that your child is ineligible for participation in an ECE program. If so, you will be notified in writing of this finding, and the evaluation process will come to a screeching halt. You should be invited to discuss the reasons for the ineligibility.

With this information under your belt, let's turn now to the discussion of goals, secrets, and skills that will help you cope effectively with the ECE program placement process.

ECE GOAL: TO ENSURE THAT SHOULD A NEED SEEM INDICATED, YOUR CHILD IS REFERRED FOR ECE EVALUATION AND THAT THE EVALUATION PROCESS OCCURS WITHIN A REASONABLE PERIOD OF TIME.

ECE GOAL: TO ENSURE THAT IF YOUR CHILD IS ELIGIBLE FOR AN ECE PROGRAM THAT YOU ARE PART OF PLANNING THE IEP AND THAT THE PLACEMENT IS APPROPRIATE.

Secrets about ECE Services

▷ **Secret # 1: The official IEP will not tell you all of the unofficial efforts the exceptional education program teacher(s) may be making on behalf of your child.**

Public Law 94-142 guidelines made in clear that all officially designated "disabled" students are supposed to have an Individual Education Plan or IEP. As stated earlier, the IEP is written and implemented primarily by the teacher(s) with whom your child will spend time in the Exceptional Child Program(s) and specialists such as the speech therapist, psychologist, or guidance counselor are often consulted when writing the IEP, which outlines goals and objectives for your child's ECE program.

Much of what is written in the IEP is a matter of regulation that they are required to routinely incorporate; dates, times, program title, goals and objectives, etc. While good teachers recognize the value of written goals, they also must try to survive the seas of burdensome paperwork so that they can spend maximum time teaching. Some will write no more than what is absolutely necessary on the Plan, but, in their dedication to the task, most Exceptional Child Education Program teachers teach many skills far beyond what is written.

Exceptional Child Education Program teachers are also notorious in their efforts to maneuver the invisible system in getting "their children" assigned to regular classroom teachers who are sensitive to and educated about the needs of exceptional children. An ECE teacher cannot say to you, "I'm trying to have your child assigned to Ms. X next year because she expects exceptional education students to achieve. She is patient and encouraging and rewards their progress and efforts. The other teachers in that grade level are irritated by exceptional education mainstreamed students." This kind of comment would be unprofessional. Therefore, the teacher quietly gets this accomplished because it is best for the child. ECE teachers of gifted students express this same kind of concern. They seek regular classroom teacher assignments with those teachers who challenge, praise, accept, and understand the gifted child.

▷ **Secret # 2: Even with complete academic, social, emotional, behavioral, and intellectual evaluations, the professionals involved still may not be sure of the "best" special education services to provide for your child.**
Many parents believe that since educators are the professionals, they should know absolutely how to heal every patient. Yet, just as medicine is not an absolute science, neither is education. Both professions deal with human beings who, no matter how much we categorize, label, study, and analyze, are all ultimately unique. A surgeon may have successfully performed the same technique thousands of times, yet one patient may inexplicably not survive. Encourage professional educators to open up and share their complete findings about your child. That may include a confession about their uncer-

tainty about the best program placement and could facilitate better program planning.

Just as skilled surgeons can lose a patient and caring parents sometimes make child-rearing errors, well-intentioned, skilled educators can make mistakes. Here are a few examples of misdiagnosis and placement errors that can occasionally occur in exceptional education:

- Culturally deprived children have been misdiagnosed as "learning disabled." Some who are culturally deprived are also learning disabled, but certainly not all.
- Emotionally disturbed children have been misplaced in learning disability programs. Some who are emotionally disturbed are also learning disabled, but again there is no necessary correlation.
- Learning disabled children have been misdiagnosed as educable mentally handicapped. Learning disabled children are *never* mentally retarded or handicapped. They must have an average or above IQ in order to qualify for the learning disabilities programs.
- Gifted children have been misdiagnosed as "purely" emotionally disturbed. Some gifted children *are* emotionally disturbed, but giftedness can fool us "normal" educators. For example, a second grade child who urinated on the classroom walls, threw paper, talked about issues well beyond a second grade level of comprehension, and generally made his teacher miserable was considered possibly EH/ED. Further investigation proved the child to be gifted. An appropriate curriculum was designed for the child and the bizarre behavior disappeared. He began enjoying school and interacting well with other children and teachers.

This list could continue, but it is sufficient to reinforce that a caring parent should be closely involved when a special program placement is being considered.

▷ **Secret #3:**

So-called "waiting lists" are illegal for children who have been evaluated and placed for exceptional child program participation. **However, without violating the law, informal waiting lists are created at various stages in the referral and eventual placement process.** For example, a regular classroom teacher may refer a child for exceptional child education evaluation and have the parent(s) sign the appropriate forms granting permission. In conversation with coordinators, administrators, and teachers in ECE, the regular classroom teacher explains that the child appears to be severely emotionally disturbed. After observation and evaluation, the group concurs with the teacher's opinion. However, all of the EH/ED programs are filled to capacity. There simply is no more room for another child.

Adding one more person to a program could measurably detract from the service that program might render to all. They know that there are no more available funds to expand the resources of the program. The spirit of the law, however, is that every child has the right to an educational program which meets her unique needs. To achieve this end, the law specifies that once a child has the IEP *officially* prescribed for an ECE program and the appropriate signatures are obtained, there can be no waiting list. A genuine dilemma exists for which those who make the law offer no solution. Those who must abide by it, the educators, will sometimes stall in scheduling the ECE parent/team conference in hopes that the family of a child currently in the program will move away, creating an opening. They certainly care about the child in question, but they also care about the others in the program who may lose quality of service if it becomes overcrowded.

This is a frustrating experience for the child who needs the program, for the regular teacher who is trying to serve the needs of all students, and for the other students in the regular classroom who may be unable to perform well if the EH/ED child is extremely disruptive. When these unofficial waiting lists occur, Child Advocate Representative activity is necessitated (see Skill #2).

▷ **Secret #4: Parents can and do influence program placement decisions.**

This secret can be your child's enemy or his savior. It's a child's enemy when parents are pushy and overbearing, and wield power to achieve an absolutely wrong—therefore cruel—program placement. For instance, the Emotionally Handicapped/Emotionally Disturbed label offends some parents who then use pressure to have a Specific Learning Disabilities program assignment instead. This is done out of ignorance and ego. Many EH/ED children have average and above IQs, but still need help with emotional, social, or behavioral disorders. By having these children misplaced in SLD, they are not getting the special services or resources that the district, the community, the state, or treatment centers have to offer. They will be receiving services for learning disabilities instead of the real help needed for their emotional handicaps. This is like applying a Band-Aid to the knee when the finger is bleeding.

Knowledge of this secret is a child's savior when a parent uses influence to prevent freak occurrences such as the placement of a gifted child, who is precocious and disruptive but not emotionally handicapped, in an EH/ED program.

▷ **Secret #5: Students who qualify for full-time SLD often remain in part-time SLD programs well beyond a reasonable time following the full-time identification.**

Children who qualify for SLD services usually begin participation in Resource (part-time) SLD. After participating in the resource program, some may qualify for full-time SLD, at which time another staffing is held and the parents give written permission for full-time placement. However, when full-time programs have no space available for a new student, a child receiving only part-time services but who qualifies for full-time services will have his "staffing"/"ECE conference" postponed until there is room in the full-time program.

This overcrowded, "wait your turn" situation also exists for other full-time and resource exceptional child programs.

Skills for Coping with ECE

▶ **Skill # 1: Request a referral for evaluative services for your child if there is evidence of academic, social, or emotional disorders or indications of giftedness.**

Parents can legitimately make this request, but the reasons should be substantial. Keep in mind that a casual interest in your child's IQ is not a reason for requesting a thorough evaluation. Such services are costly to the taxpayer and time-consuming for school personnel. They must be reserved for those children who seriously need them.

How can you know if your child has disorders, is gifted, or both? Education and honesty with yourself are your two best resources. While educating oneself about disorders takes time and self-discipline, it's more painful to be honest with oneself, to face the truths about one's children, to go beyond one's own ego, and to ultimately get them the help they need to become well-adjusted, fulfilled, happy children and adults. A heart-rending story of a kindergarten child named Stephanie illustrates the pain of being honest with ourselves.

Stephanie showed many signs of superior intelligence and simultaneously showed signs of possible learning disabilities and emotional disturbances. She was beautiful and playful, but much more immature than a "normal" kindergarten child. She was placed with a first-rate kindergarten teacher who cared about her emotional and academic progress. The teacher asked the parent for permission to refer Stephanie for evaluative services which could help identify problems and tendencies of giftedness. The mother refused, began to cry, and left the conference. Time passed, but the teacher persisted, explaining over and over the value of the testing services and that Stephanie would not be placed in any program without the mother's permission.

As the school year came to a close, the mother finally shared her fears with the teacher. She explained that since Stephanie's birth, she had felt that something was wrong. But Stephanie was her only child, and she hadn't had any other child-rearing experiences to know whether or not Stephanie had developed normally and was progressing as expected for her age. Her greatest fear was that Stephanie was mentally retarded and would be taken away from her and placed in an institution. Stephanie was definitely not retarded. This mother's fears prevented her from agreeing to evaluative testing and denied Stephanie a year's worth of needed special services. She also denied herself the peace of mind that further testing could have brought.

Oh, the pain of rearing children, and the cost of facing our worst fears! But confront them we must. Our children's welfare is too dear a price to pay for avoiding ourselves.

▶ **Skill #2: Once you have given written permission for your child to be evaluated, closely monitor the "unofficial waiting time" before an ECE conference is scheduled.**

Secret #3 reveals the existence of "unofficial waiting lists." I explained that the cause is usually that the well-intentioned educators are working within and around the laws for the best interest of the children already participating in a crowded program. The law presents them with a moral problem which they try to solve as best they can.

Of course, you also care about the other children, and you understand their dilemma. But you are the only A/R your child has. You simply must keep gentle pressure on these "unofficial waiting lists," stimulating the professionals to find a creative solution for all.

A simple way to do this is to persist. I do not advise pushy, aggressive, or hostile behavior. The old "squeaky wheel gets the grease" trick is sufficient. Politely ask on a regular basis, "When will the conference about test results be scheduled?" This persistence often results in a conference being held sooner than if you waited quietly for something to happen.

▶ **Skill #3: Ask to be part of planning the Individual Education Program.**

Parents should be included in the planning process at the ECE conference. However, much planning occurs beforehand. You may wish to be part of the initial stages of planning an IEP for a program(s) placement. This will give you an opportunity to hear professionals discuss plans for your child's future at school. Listening will add to your insight. But be sensitive to the use of the professionals' time. Remember that they serve many other children as well as yours.

▶ **Skill #4: Request to visit the recommended exceptional child program(s) before you grant written permission for program placement.**

In order to attend some exceptional child programs, participants must travel on buses to another school. In some cases, a parent must compare the cost to the child of the time lost in the regular classroom to the cost of nonparticipation in the ECE program. For example, some gifted programs provide a two-hour service per week to students from several schools. A third grade child might spend three hours a week including travel and participation in the program. If the program provides extraordinary services beyond the regular classroom and your child copes well with change and travel, then you may wish to permit her participation. However, 36 school weeks × 3 hours per week = 108 hours of instruction and travel. These are precious hours, especially if your child participates in this kind of program for several years; 108 hours per year × 5 years = 540 hours of instruction and travel.

Do you see the potential impact of your decision? Visiting the recommended programs will add to your data for better educational planning.

▶ **Skill #5: Study the suggested mainstreaming and "pull-out" plans for the continuity of your child's day and curriculum.** (Chapter 7 will help you with this skill.)

I've seen children who were "pulled out" of the regular classroom for several programs. Every day they were expected to perform in the regular classroom program according to all of the criteria established for the children who stayed in that classroom program all day. Imagine receiving an F in biology, having never attended class because you were pulled out of your biology class to study history in which you didn't get a grade because it was a special course. Ridiculous, no? Let's consider the story of Doug.

Doug was in second grade. Every day he was in Resource SLD for 45 minutes, remedial reading for 30 minutes, and speech for 10 minutes. He missed 1 hour and 25 minutes of the regular class time in addition to the time it took him to travel to and from these other classes. Let's add 15 minutes for travel and interruption of concentration, and we have 1 hour and 40 minutes in three separate increments that Doug was out of the regular classroom each day. What did he miss while he was gone? Reading? Math? Spelling?

This story emphasizes the necessity for an EP-A/R to know exactly how much time is spent where, and how the regular classroom teacher plans to help your child achieve reasonable expectations in relationship to his schedule. Mainstream and pull-out knowledge is essential.

A Final Word about Exceptional Child Education Programs

There are many fine aspects of Exceptional Child Education Programs. I have rarely met a teacher in these programs who was not highly qualified both personally and professionally. The secrets emerging from ECE tend to be *primarily* related to mechanics of management.

The five skills listed above will help you better use the services of the Exceptional Child Education Public School Programs or Special Student Services to the advantage of your child. I've attended many "staffings" in which parents without knowledge of the program, without trying to understand the IEP, without carefully appreciating how the child's daily instructional schedule would change, and without reviewing the mainstreaming plan, would grant written permission for program(s) participation, naively delegating their EP-A/R responsibilities to others.

The exceptional child personnel are not deviously plotting to prevent you from learning these things. In fact, at ECE conferences they are generally eager to answer all of your questions. So ask! You're representing your child's best interests and planning his educational future.

PROGRAMS FOR THE EDUCATIONALLY DISADVANTAGED (ECIA CHAPTER I)

Sometimes a child has learning problems that are not severe enough to meet ECE criteria but which still adversely affect his ability to learn. Such a child might be referred to a "Chapter I" program for supplementary help. Chapter I programs are remedial programs designed to meet the needs of "disadvantaged" children. These programs are federally funded and regulated under Chapter I of the Education Consolidation and Improvement Act of 1981 (ECIA). But do these programs actually accomplish the ends for which they were designed? To answer this question we must first take a look at what might be considered the birth of federal legislation affecting public education (traditionally funded and regulated by the states)—the Elementary and Secondary Education Act of 1965 (ESEA). It came into the world kicking and screaming and creating much controversy, none of which has abated. Essentially, this act provided large sums of federal dollars to the states to be filtered down to the local school districts to improve the health and education of children of lower-income families, of those living in economically depressed urban and rural areas, and of children living in sparsely populated areas. Who could argue with such a worthy cause? There are studies upon studies that claim a positive relationship between economic deprivation and poor academic performance. When the school districts receive these funds, they must target them toward the schools within that district with the required percentage of low-income families.

Whew! We have finally reached the schools. But wait! Hold on! How was the census taken to target the schools within the district meeting the low-income family requirements? Simple, the schools that had a specified percent of free- and reduced-lunch participants were nominated the chosen ones to receive the educational monies for programs for disadvantaged children. These programs generally address the needs of children with problems in reading and math, particularly reading. After the school has the programs, criteria and guidelines based on educational need are applied to select the students who can participate—presumably the disadvantaged children at which the ESEA was targeted.

Does this mean that children in wealthy or middle income families don't have reading problems? Well, if they do, and they want this federal help, they'd better go to schools where the required percentage of children are on the free- and reduced-lunch program. Aren't these families taxpayers too? More correctly, aren't they the families paying the taxes that support federal program assistance for the lower-income families? Oh well, we rationalize, the wealthier and middle-income families can afford tutors. Let's just wait one minute here. First, families who don't qualify for free or reduced lunch are not necessarily wealthy or even middle-income. Often their income is just slightly above meeting the program qualifications.

Second, to qualify for free or reduced lunch, a parent/guardian merely completes an application and submits it to the school with his signature affirming that his statements about income, number of dependents, etc., are all truthful. An administrator (or appointee) in each school is responsible for reviewing every application.

When I was an administrator, I sat up many nights with literally stacks of applications, as did many of my colleagues. Before approving them for the program, I verified that each applicant, *according to his statements* on the form, met the criteria for participation. This is certainly counting on the honesty of literally thousands of people who are using our tax dollars. I have had several parents, enraged that they were not approved for free lunch, who blamed the school system for not telling them in advance what salary they had to claim in order to qualify. Yes, auditors do spot-check the validity of the applications, but the majority of applications are not investigated.

So what do we have? We have schools receiving federal dollars based upon numbers of approved free- or reduced-lunch applications which, for the most part, are not investigated and unverified as to their accuracy. And we have taxpayers supporting this farce who do not receive the benefits of free-lunch programs because of their income and their honesty and whose children, if not attending a targeted school, will not receive the benefits of these federal dollars, even if they are educationally "disadvantaged."

To continue this tragicomedy, ESEA of 1965 was repealed and replaced with the Education Consolidation and Improvement Act of 1981. What does this change mean on a long-range basis as it directly relates to our children? It is too soon to tell. Its immediate effect has essentially *not* changed the remedial programs for our children, which fall under Chapter I of the new act, or the way schools are targeted for the monies. Its main impact thus far has been on the way states and districts receive money from the federal government.

ECIA Chapter I—Are the Programs Helpful?

Let's focus our attention on a few realities of the programs funded through ECIA Chapter I as they affect children. When dealing with Chapter I programs, your goal as an EP-A/R will be:

TO ENSURE THAT YOUR CHILD IS PARTICIPATING IN EDUCATIONALLY BENEFICIAL PROGRAMS AND IS SPENDING PRIME INSTRUCTIONAL HOURS IN MEANINGFUL ACTIVITY.

Secrets about ECIA Chapter I Programs

▷ **Secret # 1: ECIA Chapter I program guidelines permit employment of instructional personnel (aides, paraprofessionals, assistants) who can have as little as a high school education.**
Example: A child who is two grade levels behind in reading and demonstrates on standardized tests that she is academically below grade level expectations could qualify for an ECIA Chapter I Basics remedial reading program. Irony of ironies, this child, who is often economically disadvantaged and who struggles academically, is assigned a program which removes her for a period of 30 to 45 minutes per day from the class of a specifically trained and certified teacher and places her with an assistant teacher, an aide, or paraprofessional

who may have as little as a high school degree. One might reasonably expect that children with serious reading difficulties would be assigned to specialists who have had years of training. No, indeed. Instead, children with academic problems are often assigned to those less trained than the teacher from whose room they are removed. Of course, there is a fully certificated Head Teacher who is responsible for school-based Chapter I program coordination. The Head Teacher is supposed to plan and monitor the instructional activities and methods of the "assistants," a title which varies within states. Usually, the Head Teacher directly teaches a fair share of the students in the program. There are some educational approaches which permit the Head Teacher to become involved with all of her ECIA students. But in many other situations, some students are instructed by the Head Teacher and some by the assistants. Who would you want for your child, the Head Teacher or an assistant? Before you answer, read on.

▷ **Secret #2: Occasionally the performance of the ECIA teacher (assistant or head) is better than that of the regular classroom teacher (regardless of level of education).**

An instructor plans, evaluates, tests, instructs, follows curriculum/program guidelines, and helps your child achieve specific objectives and goals. In essence, the instructor is the conveyance of any program. Basal reading series, equipment, time, and supplementary texts are all resources, but they are not essentially the curriculum. The curriculum, hidden and obvious, is delivered by the instructor who uses the available resources. Some teachers use resources more effectively than others. I have observed that remedial students blessed with outstanding ECIA Chapter I instructors didn't lose additional academic ground, as was usually the case, when their classroom teacher was unacceptable.

So don't answer too quickly the question, "Who is the most qualified to teach my child, the Head Teacher, the assistant, or the classroom teacher?" One, all, or none might be acceptable.

▷ **Secret #3: Some children who receive the services of Chapter I ECIA "Score no higher on achievement tests years later than do their peers who were eligible for such services but did not receive them," states Dr. Richard Culyer, Professor of Education, in his article, "Chapter I Programs: Problems and Promising Solutions."**

In a 1983 article by Susan Kuntz of Syracuse University and Richard Lyczak of the RMC Research Corporation, they reported that, in their study which examined the academic losses and gains of Title I (Chapter I) students over the summer months, substantial losses occured. Does this mean that the program during the year was ineffective? Does it mean that if the child didn't have ECIA Chapter I instruction during the year that the losses would be still greater? Further research is needed here.

In another study by Robert L. Ziomek and William J. Schoenenberger of the Des Moines, Iowa, Independent Community School District there were some idiosyncratic results. This study focused upon the relationship between attendance and student achievement. Grades 2 through 6 in a large midwestern school district were selected to participate. While the results of the study indicated that program attendance is positively related to achievement gains, in some individual cases high gains were associated with low program attendance and in others high attendance was associated with substantial losses. This is definitely worth further study.

Ruth Weinstock, Senior Project Director with the Educational Facilities Laboratories of the Academy for Educational Development in New York City, wrote an article published in May 1984 about the Kansas City, Kansas, Title I (Chapter I) program. This Chapter I program uses a learning center method of instruction and it showed substantial student gains.

The learning center has individual carrels with tape players, headphones, felt-tip markers and other necessary materials. Each center or lab is staffed by a teacher and an aide.

What do these and other studies with conflicting results mean to you as a parent? It can certainly be confusing. It means that an EP-A/R must take time to understand the ECIA Chapter I programs available in your child's school and district. After compliance with federal and state requirements, many guidelines for implementing these programs are left to the discretion of the individual school districts. Let's consider in broad terms the way in which a rather typical Chapter I program services students.

Children participating in Chapter I programs are usually "pulled out" of the regular classroom for 30 to 45 minutes per day. A normal school year has approximately 179 days. Considering opening, closing, and testing days, plus the unusually high rate of absenteeism among these students, due to sanctioned absences such as class field trips, school assemblies, scheduling conflicts, picture days, etc., and unsanctioned absences such as illness, a reasonable estimate of available instructional days in Chapter I is approximately 150.

Consider next the time factor. In the "pull-out" programs, a 30-minute- to 45-minute-per-day instruction period minus travel to and from the regular class and lost time in concentration for beginning and ending tasks can total as much as a 15 minute loss or more per period. Subsequently the instructional time is reduced to 15 to 30 minutes instead of the originally planned 30 to 45 minutes per day.

150 days × 15 minutes per day = 37½ hours per week
150 days × 30 minutes per day = 75 hours per year

Do you see the problem? Is it likely that a child with serious academic difficulties can be helped in piecemeal fashion by people who lack training in the specialized areas of need? There is evidence that tells us that long-range benefits are negligible, if there are any at all. But, after you consider the quality of the programs your district provides, your child's needs and scheduled time, you will be better prepared to make an informed decision.

▷ **Secret # 4: Some regular classroom teachers illegally supplant the regular classroom instructional reading or math program with Chapter I remedial reading or math instruction which is designed to be only supplementary.**

This means for example that children participating in ECIA for supplementary reading instruction often do not receive in the regular teacher's classroom the amount or quality of reading instruction required or recommended by state and local boards of education. The concept of supplementary reading is just that! It is intended to support, shoreup, add to an already existing reading program in the classroom.

Harry N. Chandler, associate editor of *The Journal of Learning Disabilities*, stated in a 1982 article that "The most important guideline, and the one most often ignored, is that Title I (Chapter I) programs must 'Supplement, Not Supplant.'" Some teachers explain that they just don't have the time to teach all of their students, and the ECIA students are getting reading instruction each day anyway. These teachers are missing the point. Remedial students need assistance "in addition to" the classroom instruction, not "instead of." Apparently, these teachers don't concern themselves with the ECIA requirements or the academic welfare of their remedial students.

▷ **Secret # 5: Many classroom teachers view Chapter I as a place to send children to get them out of their rooms and as a rationale for dismissing their own instructional accountability.**

Sam's experiences illustrate the cruel reality of this secret. A seriously emotionally handicapped child, Sam had for two years participated 45 minutes a day in an ECIA reading program. Oh, yes, he qualified according to the standardized test criteria and other guidelines, but he was also intelligently superior and read extremely well. This placement error might have occurred because his emotional problems prevented him from making an effort on the qualifying tests. Consequently, he scored poorly enough for program eligibility. Didn't the Chapter I assistant notice that he read well, with comprehension, inflection, and verbal ability?

The assistant's comment to me was, "Yes, he does read well. To be honest, he's in my class because he is such a problem for the regular teacher that she needs a break from him. The other students learn more when he's out of her class. In my class, he's here only forty-five minutes, and there are only six children. While difficult, he's a little more controllable in here."

After concerned intervention, Sam was removed from ECIA and had a special education program planned to meet his needs. He began to get the help he needed, help that obviously had nothing to do with reading skill.

It's much more complicated for a regular classroom teacher to have a child placed in an exceptional child program than in an ECIA Chapter I program because the ECE qualifying procedures are much more detailed. Therefore, some teachers take the most convenient, quickest route to get the child out of the classroom.

▷ **Secret #6: A child in a Chapter I class obviously is missing something in the regular curriculum during his absence.**

This isn't a "true" secret as such, because it is common sense that a child can only be in one place at a time. Often teachers do not coordinate the classroom and ECIA curricula. Children who are already academically "behind" in reading may now become "behind" in math or science, because they may miss those subjects when they attend ECIA classes. Each child can have a schedule that includes all facets of the curriculum, but the teachers must make the effort to accomplish that task.

▷ **Secret #7: Children who are below grade level in reading will probably be given reading texts on their level of instruction, but in other subject areas they will usually be given texts consistent with the grade to which they are assigned.**

For example, a third grade child two reading levels below grade level may be using a first grade reading series in ECIA Chapter I and in the regular class program. However, even though everyone has identified that the child cannot read beyond first grade level, he is given third grade texts in English, spelling, science, health, and social studies. This is common practice. Can this child read the science text well enough to follow directions and complete assignments? The answer is, sadly, no.

▷ **Secret #8: Some identified SLD children are placed only in Chapter I programs because parents fear the "stigma and disgrace" of having a child in a special education program.**

SLD participants may also legally attend ECIA Chapter I. This plan works well for some children. However, because some parents will not agree to an SLD placement, other children attend *only* ECIA when in fact they have identified learning disabilities. It is a tragic error to place a learning-disabled child with an assistant ECIA teacher who has minimal training compared to that of the SLD specialist who has the resources and expertise to help learning-disabled children. The loss to the child in such cases is incalculable.

▷ **Secret #9: Training programs for teachers give credit toward recertification when the teacher merely attends.**

Physical attendance, not proof of achievement, is usually all that is required for teachers in in-service programs to receive credit. This secret holds true not only for many in-service training programs for ECIA Chapter I teachers but for those of regular classroom teachers as well.

Skills for Coping with ECIA Chapter I Programs

▶ **Skill # 1: Ask about the qualifications of the Chapter I teacher to whom your child may be assigned.**
Remember that the degree of education is important, but is not the sole deciding factor as to whether or not to permit your child to attend. This is only additional data to help you provide the best educational plan for your child.

▶ **Skill # 2: Before granting written permission for your child's participation, visit the recommended Chapter I program and teacher(s) to whom your child would be assigned.**
This is well worth 30 minutes of your time. Remember that your child will spend roughly 38 to 75 hours a year in this program, hours taken from the regular classroom. Long-range academic achievement may be affected by your decision.

▶ **Skill # 3: Discuss with the regular classroom teacher exactly what your child will miss while attending Chapter I classes. Compare the relative value of what is missed to the value of the ECIA class. Together, consider ways to help your child compensate for or adjust to the curriculum changes.** Adjust the curriculum to the child!

▶ **Skill # 4: Be certain that if you agree to Chapter I remedial assistance, your child will continue to receive instruction in that same subject area in the regular classroom.**
For example, a Chapter I child in the remedial reading program should have reading instruction in the regular classroom as well; a double service should be given.

▶ **Skill #5: Ask about the grade level of materials used for each subject area.**

Your interest is, "Are all of the texts on my child's instructional level?" "If not, why not?" "What are the grade level texts needed for each subject?"

▶ **Skill #6: In consultation with appropriate school personnel, analyze all placement options recommended for your child and make decisions based solely upon your child's welfare.**

Rule out your ego, the teacher's ego, or what friends and neighbors might think. This skill is also essential when considering an ECE program(s) placement.

A Final Word about ECIA Chapter I Programs

After reviewing many studies, and from my experience, I am comfortable recommending an ECIA placement only after a parent is absolutely aware of his/her child's needs and of the value of a particular school's program before giving permission for attendance in one of these programs. Parents should visit the program suggested and review the instructors' qualifications and performance. The regular classroom instruction should provide instruction *in addition* to the remedial and purely supplementary ECIA Chapter I program. Some programs in some districts have a lot to offer, others can be a tragic waste of a child's valuable time. As a teacher and administrator I experienced both situations for my students within the same district. In one school, several of my remedial students had tremendously improved academic gains which were obvious through observation of daily assignments as well as through test results. In another school where the program was implemented less effectively the results were in keeping with the unacceptability of the instructional program. If you relocate within your district, which forces your child to attend a different school, and your child is currently enrolled in a Chapter I program in the first school, it will be necessary to be as thorough in your review of the next school's Chapter I program(s) as you were when your child first entered.

SUMMARY
EXCEPTIONAL CHILD EDUCATION PROGRAMS

ECE GOAL: TO ENSURE THAT SHOULD A NEED SEEM INDI-
CATED, YOUR CHILD IS REFERRED FOR ECE EVALUATION
AND THAT THE EVALUATION PROCESS OCCURS WITHIN A
REASONABLE PERIOD OF TIME.

ECE GOAL: TO ENSURE THAT IF YOUR CHILD IS ELIGIBLE
FOR AN ECE PROGRAM THAT YOU ARE PART OF PLANNING
THE IEP AND THAT THE PLACEMENT IS APPROPRIATE.

Secrets about ECE Programs

Secret # 1: The official IEP that you may read will not tell you all of the unofficial efforts the exceptional education program teacher(s) may be making on behalf of your child.

Secret # 2: Even with complete academic, social, emotional, behavioral, and intellectual evaluations, the professionals involved still may not be sure of the "best" special education services to provide for your child.

Secret # 3: Informal waiting lists are created at various stages in the referral and eventual placement process.

Secret # 4: Parents can and do influence program placement decisions. (But it is not a secret that parents have the final decision, to agree or not to agree to any program placement.)

Secret # 5: Students who qualify for full-time SLD often remain in part-time SLD programs well beyond a reasonable time following the full-time identification. This holds true for other part-time–full-time ECE programs.

Skills for Coping with ECE Programs

Skill # 1: Request a referral for evaluative services for your child if there is evidence of academic, social, or emotional disorders or indications of giftedness.

Skill # 2: Once you have given written permission for your child to be evaluated, closely monitor the "unofficial waiting time" before a "staffing" or an "ECE conference" is scheduled.

Skill # 3: Ask to be part of planning the IEP.

Skill # 4: Request to visit the recommended exceptional child program before you grant written permission for program placement.

Skill # 5: Study the suggested mainstreaming and "pull-out" plans for continuity of your child's day and curriculum.

ECIA Chapter I Programs

GOAL: TO ENSURE THAT YOUR CHILD IS PARTICIPATING IN EDUCATIONALLY BENEFICIAL PROGRAMS AND IS SPENDING PRIME INSTRUCTIONAL HOURS IN MEANINGFUL ACTIVITY.

Secrets about ECIA Chapter I Programs

Secret # 1: ECIA Chapter I program guidelines permit employment of instructional personnel (aides, paraprofessionals, assistants) who can have as little as a high school education.

Secret # 2: Occasionally the performance of the ECIA teacher (assistant or head) is "better" than that of the regular classroom teacher (regardless of level of education).

Secret # 3: Some children who receive the services of Chapter I ECIA "score no higher on achievement tests years later than do their peers who were eligible for such services but did not receive them."

Secret # 4: Some regular classroom teachers illegally supplant the regular classroom instructional reading or math program with Chapter I remedial reading or math instruction which is designed to be only supplementary.

Secret # 5: Many classroom teachers view Chapter I as a place to send children to get them out of their rooms and as a rationale for dismissing their own instructional accountability.

Secret # 6: A child in a Chapter I class obviously is missing something in the regular classroom during his absence.

Secret # 7: Children who are below grade level in reading will probably be given "reading" texts on their level of instruction, but in other subject areas they will usually be given texts consistent with the grade to which they are assigned.

Secret # 8: Some identified SLD children are placed only in Chapter I programs because parents fear the "stigma and disgrace" of having a child in a special education program.

Secret # 9: Training programs for teachers give credit toward recertification when the teacher merely attends.

Skills for Coping with ECIA Chapter I Programs

Skill # 1: Ask about the qualifications of the Chapter I teacher to whom your child may be assigned.

Skill # 2: Before granting written permission for your child's participation, visit the recommended Chapter I program and teacher(s).

Skill # 3: Discuss with the regular classroom teacher exactly what your child will miss while attending Chapter I classes. Compare the relative value of what is missed to the value of the ECIA class. Together, consider ways to help your child compensate for or adjust to the curriculum changes.

Skill # 4: Be certain that if you agree to Chapter I remedial assistance, your child will continue to receive instruction in that same subject area in the regular classroom.

Skill # 5: Ask about the grade level of materials used for each subject area.

Skill # 6: In consultation with appropriate school personnel, analyze all placement options recommended for your child. Make decisions based solely upon your child's welfare. This skill applies to ECE programs as well.

MOVING FORWARD ...

The next chapter may be the most critical chapter in this book. It will require the use of many of the skills in all of the preceding chapters. Keep reading!

7
Your Child's Daily Schedule: An Important Key to Achievement

We have thus far considered the Child Advocate/Representative and Educational Planning services we afford our children when we effectively manage conferences, enrollment procedures, classroom reassignments, extra program services, and "helping at school." We have come to realize that we are not powerless, and that the educational institution does not necessarily have to be our benevolent dictator. We turn now to our final public school EP-A/R issue, one which is at least as important as, if not more critical than, all of the preceding concerns—Instructional Time Management (ITM).

Why should parents concern themselves with Instructional Time Management, something unfamiliar and potentially uncomfortable? Does school time need to be controlled by parents? Don't the teachers, principals, county-level administrators, and state-level administrators manage that time? Why should parents take valuable time out of their already busy days to learn about and control instructional time for their children? Many parents labor under the misconception that if a child goes to school every day, or on most days, she is getting the time needed to learn specific subjects such as reading and math. Oh, what a wonderful but potentially dangerous illusion.

If your child is having difficulty mastering particular subjects or skills, if achievement records indicate poor or slow progress, and/or if her social conduct records reflect difficulties with adjustment to the public school situation, then take a few minutes to understand her daily school schedule. While the schedule may not be the critical primary source of your child's difficulties, it is only common sense to first determine whether or not she is even being given opportunities to achieve. It would be far better to use preventive medicine and review your child's daily schedule before problems exist than to wait for problems to develop. A child's daily schedule should be routinely written at the beginning of every school year and updated as the schedule changes. It sounds ludicrous, doesn't it, that schools would expect children to excel in subjects which they are not given time to learn, and then award them failing grades for the crime of not achieving. Ludicrous, yes, but tragically true.

ITM is defined here as the way in which the state, the district/county, the school, the parents, and the individual teachers manage the available instructional time of every school year, month, and day. Managing instructional time may at first appear to be beyond the control of Educational Planners. However, there are several "time factors" which are manageable and, therefore, are changeable and within a parent's control.

TIME FACTORS AFFECTING INSTRUCTION AND ACHIEVEMENT:

1. The length of the school year (the number of days per year designated for student attendance)
2. The number of days a student actually attends school

3. The length of the school day (the number of hours per day children are taught at school)

4. The specific number of *minutes* per day, week, or month required or recommended by the state or district for each subject

5. The specific number of *minutes* per day or week the individual teachers schedule for each subject

6. The actual number of minutes per day or week the teacher productively uses the scheduled subject area time

7. The actual number of minutes per day, per week, per year that students spend actively participating in and "engaged" with a particular subject or related specific task

8. The actual time students spend actively participating in and "successfully engaged" with a particular subject or related specific task (There is a vast difference between *applying* oneself and *successfully* doing so.)

These eight time factors may directly affect in varying degrees the academic achievement of your child and indirectly influence his social adjustment. Common sense and numerous professional studies confirm that the amount of time spent in learning is of critical importance in determining a child's achievement. Logically, then, the first prerequisite to achievement is availability of instructional time. The allocation of that time is initiated by first scheduling the school year, day, and time for each subject. The nationwide school year average is approximately 179 school days per year. The nationwide average length of the school day is approximately 5 hours. Your child is probably attending a school which is reasonably close to these two time factors. If there is a serious inadequacy of instructional time pertaining to the number of school days per year and instructional hours per day, then it is advisable to contact your local school board for further discussion. In some cases you may need to form a group of concerned parents, an issue which I discuss in further detail in

Chapter 10. If you are satisfied with the time schedules for school days and hours per day, then begin considering the other six time factors. Once again, we will begin our analytical endeavor by first establishing our EP-A/R goal for Instructional Time Management (ITM).

ITM GOAL: TO REVIEW THE APPROPRIATENESS OF AMOUNTS OF TIME SCHEDULED FOR EACH SUBJECT AREA FOR YOUR CHILD AND TO DETERMINE THE QUALITY OF THAT SCHEDULED IN-STRUCTIONAL TIME IN ORDER TO ASSURE THAT YOUR CHILD HAS THE BEST POSSIBLE OPPORTUNITY TO MASTER THE REQUIRED CURRICULUM.

While the following secrets and skills may unsettle your sense of security about school curricula, they also can provide you with a new and realistic vision of the role of an Educational Planner (EP) and the tools necessary to fulfill that role. With your commitment to the task, they will help you obtain your ITM goal.

INSTRUCTIONAL TIME MANAGEMENT SECRETS

▷ **Secret #1: The fact that your child goes to school every day does not necessarily mean that he is receiving enough instructional time or quality time to master the required curriculum.**

▷ **Secret #2: Often the instructional schedule of individual teachers varies drastically within the same school and grade level.**

A 1977 teacher evaluation study conducted by M. Dishaw under the auspices of the San Francisco Far West Laboratory for Educational Research and Development reported that time actually scheduled per day "for second grade math ranged from a low of 24 minutes to a high of 61 minutes, and for second grade reading from 32 minutes to 131 minutes." I found this to be true in all grade levels not only between schools but within schools as well. Can you predict the achievement level of your child if he receives half or less than half the instructional time that other children receive in the same grade level?

▷ **Secret #3:**
Many states, districts, and schools have established specific amounts of time for subjects such as reading/language arts and math. **Even with specific time requirements, some teachers do not schedule instructional time following those requirements.**

Permit me to share a personal experience which dramatically illustrates the awful truth of this secret. During the third quarter of a school year when I was teaching second grade, a new teacher was assigned to relieve the overcrowded classroom conditions in second and third grades. The principal decided (for some unknown reason) to reassign practically all of the second and third graders to different classrooms. After these reassignments, I had, as did the other teachers, approximately four of my original students left in the class.

There we were, practically beginning fourth quarter, with a new class. We teachers decided that our frustration and disorientation could be partially overcome by exchanging student achievement records and familiarizing ourselves with each child's academic and social performances. We scheduled conferences to exchange the records of our former students and to receive the records of our new students.

It was during these conferences that I was thrown into dismal shock about my colleagues. I gave them detailed information about each child concerning their instructional time schedules, what had been achieved thus far, and written future goals and objectives. However, not one of those teachers strictly followed required county instructional time schedule allotments. Not one gave me well-documented student achievement information about the "basic skills" which were required by the county and state. Not one had clearly identified future objectives for each child.

Fourth quarter was upon me and I had to begin to determine if these children had mastered all of the second grade required "basic skills." As a direct result of this experience, I became determined to get involved in school administration. Surely something could be done to ensure children of at least the right to equal instructional time and opportunities to learn.

During my administrative years, it was a constant effort to supervise scheduled instructional time allocations. Many teachers consciously or subconsciously resisted following state and county guidelines.

▷ **Secret #4: Even when some teachers' schedules reflect the required amount of time per subject, that scheduled time is often abused.**

For example:

• Permitting students to work unsuccessfully on tasks for unlimited amounts of time without assisting them. With appropriate assistance the student could have spent the time successfully completing the task. Students can be "busy" successfully completing assignments or "busy" doing everything incorrectly because of lack of understanding.

• Deciding that he is not in the "mood" to teach and giving the students ditto sheets to color, films to watch which have no relationship to the instructional subject area or objectives, or an overabundance of free-time activity.

• Presenting material to students haphazardly because of the lack of preparation and planning.

• Strongly emphasizing "instructional spontaneity" because of weak classroom organizational skills and management techniques.

• Providing inadequate discipline and, therefore, greatly minimizing opportunities for students to concentrate and academically achieve.

▷ **Secret # 5:**
Because of these abuses and others, **the time your child spends "successfully engaged" may be minimal.** "Successful engagement" is defined here as, "Involvement with tasks by a student which leads to mastery of those tasks, often as a result of corrective feedback by the teacher (or other adult, or peer student) before continued errors reinforce (support) unacceptable learned behavior."

For example: "Engaged Behavior": 2+2=7, 2+2=7, 2+2=7, 2+2=7, 2+2=7. "Successfully Engaged Behavior": 2+2=7/correction/2+2=4, 2+2=4, 2+2=4.

As Coach Vince Lombardi said, "Practice doesn't make perfect. Perfect practice makes perfect." If your child brings home school assignments (not tests) indicating that he continues to make the same kinds of repeated errors, then the EP-A/R skills in this chapter are for you.

▷ **Secret # 6: If the teacher does not have a well-outlined daily and weekly schedule, no matter what the reason given you, your child's time is being wasted.**
Every instructor should have long- and short-range objectives and goals which can be obtained only by first beginning with appropriate instructional time allocations. Essentially, instruction cannot occur if class time is not dedicated to that end.

When requesting your child's specific daily schedule, you may get responses from the teacher ranging from, "I'm a creative, flexible teacher who takes advantage of the teachable moment. Therefore, I don't have a written schedule," to "Of course, I would be happy to show you my class schedule and to complete an individual one for you and your child." Because of special student service programs that many children attend, students within the same classroom may have vastly different schedules. It is an excellent idea for parents to have a copy of their child's instructional schedule. This helps them monitor appropriate uses of instructional time.

If a teacher is threatened by your request for a written copy of your child's schedule, refer to the EP-A/R skills for effective conferencing given in Chapter 3.

WHY INSTRUCTIONAL TIME MANAGEMENT IS NECESSARY

Before reviewing the skills necessary to achieve an understanding of how to cope creatively with Instructional Time Management, let's take a brief look at a 1982 report entitled "Time Spent In Learning: Implications from Research," written by Janet H. Caldwell, William G. Huitt, and Anne O. Graeber, and published by the University of Chicago Press. This report and the accompanying table illustrate the significance of parental involvement with a child's daily schedule.

[The table] shows that in an average elementary situation the school year is 180 days, with students attending school 160 days. Each school day of about 5 hours includes about 2 hours of reading/language arts instruction and about 45 minutes of math instruction. Students are engaged about 60 percent of the allocated time, spending about 72 minutes on task for reading/language arts and about 27 minutes on task for math. They are working successfully on relevant academic tasks for about half this time, about 36 minutes each day for reading/language arts and 14 minutes each day for math. During an average school year, students thus have about 96 hours of academic learning time in reading/language arts and about 37 hours in math.

In the low-average situation, students attend school an average of 150 days and each school day is only 4½ hours. Allocated time is only 90 minutes for reading/language arts and 30 minutes for math each day. The engagement rate is low, about 45 percent. Student engaged time is 41 minutes for reading/language arts and 14 minutes for math, compared with 72 and 27 minutes in the average situation. If students are working successfully on relevant academic tasks only 30 percent of the time, then academic learning time is reduced to 12 minutes for reading/language arts and 4 minutes for math, less than one-third as much as in the average case. Over the year, students have only 30 hours of academic learning time in reading/language arts and 10 hours in math.

In the high-average case, the attendance year is 170 days and the length of the school day is 5½ hours. Daily allocated times are 2½ hours for reading/language arts and 1 hour for math. Engagement rates are 75 percent. Student engaged times are about 113 minutes for reading/language arts and 45 minutes for math. Students are working successfully on relevant academic tasks for 70 percent of the time, about 79 minutes for reading/language arts and 32 minutes for math. Over the year, students thus have 224 hours of academic learning time in reading/language arts and 90 hours in math. This is more than twice as much academic learning time as in the average case and more than six times as much as in the low-average case.

Using the table, consider the two extremes and probable achievement differential between low average time and high average time. If your child received only 300 hours a year of reading/language arts instruction as opposed to 595 hours per year, would the 295 hour difference in instructional time affect her achievement? How would it affect her achievement over a period of several years?

TABLE: COMPARISONS OF TIME AVAILABLE FOR SCHOOLING ACROSS VARIOUS SITUATIONS

	Low Average		Average		High Average	
	Daily	Yearly	Daily	Yearly	Daily	Yearly
School year (1)	...	180 days	...	180 days	...	180 days
Attendance year (1)	...	150 days	...	160 days	...	170 days
School day (2)	4½ hr	675 hr	5 hr	800 hr	5½ hr	935 hr
Allocated time (3):						
Reading/language arts	90 min	225 hr	2 hr	320 hr	2½ hr	425 hr
Mathematics	30 min	75 hr	45 min	120 hr	1 hr	170 hr
Basic skills total	120 min	300 hr	165 min	440 hr	3½ hr	595 hr
Engagement rate (2) (%):	45		60		75	
Student engaged time:						
Reading/language arts	41 min	100 hr	72 min	192 hr	113 min	320 hr
Mathematics	14 min	34 hr	27 min	72 hr	45 min	128 hr
Basic skills total	55 min	134 hr	99 min	264 hr	158 min	448 hr
Academic learning time (4)(%):	(30)		(50)		(70)	
Reading/language arts	12 min	30 hr	36 min	96 hr	79 min	224 hr
Mathematics	4 min	10 hr	14 min	37 hr	32 min	90 hr
Basic skills total	16 min	40 hr	50 min	133 hr	111 min	314 hr

NOTE: Averages and standard deviations are obtained from data reported in: Kemmerer 1979(1), Brady et al. 1977 (2), Dishaw 1977b(3), and Fisher et al. 1978(4). May 1982.

Now you have arrived at a moment of truth! If one recognizes the impact that time management could make upon a child's lifelong achievement, then one must do something to maximize her chances to receive the amount and the quality of instructional time needed to achieve. You'll be pleasantly surprised at the ease with which the ITM coping skills can be mastered. They are possibly the least difficult EP-A/R skills to learn in this entire book, and yet they can deliver great benefits to your child.

Participating in the management of her daily instructional schedule will take you and your child a step beyond being victims of an impersonal system.

The Educational Planner's first task, as previously mentioned, is to review the number of school days per year and the number of school hours per day. If these are acceptable, then the second undertaking is to learn of your child's daily and weekly instructional schedule. Remember that children within the same classroom can have schedules that vary drastically. While you may be interested in the class schedule, what you need is your child's individual one. This beginning awareness of the currently scheduled uses of time will precede the analysis of the quality of that time.

INSTRUCTIONAL TIME MANAGEMENT SKILLS

▶ **Skill #1: Obtain a written schedule of your child's total day.**

For your conference with your child's teacher, you may wish to use the two optional daily schedule forms provided for your convenience in Chapter 8 (see pages 192–97). These are simple forms with the days of the week, times of the school day, and spaces for the subjects taught during those times. You and the teacher may wish to complete one of these forms. However, any schedule form will serve if it gives you a complete, neat, concrete, overall picture of your child's instructional day.

As recommended previously, your child's daily schedule should be routinely obtained from his teacher(s) at the beginning of every school year as a preventive measure. This written schedule should be updated if your child's actual schedule changes during the school year.

The teacher may request time to complete a daily schedule form for you and give it to you a day or so later. Whatever is mutually acceptable to those involved at the conference would be fine. The point is to have a written schedule of your child's complete school day, including instructional time and all other noninstructional activities, such as lunch. Every school minute should be accounted for on the schedule.

Samples of completed schedule forms are also included in Chapter 8. As you review the samples, note that the written schedule provides a wonderful picture of the way a child spends instructional time. You can then total that time per day, per week, and per year to determine the appropriateness of the amount.

You can learn about your school district's and state's instructional subject-area-time guidelines, requirements, or recommendations by asking the school principal or elementary school directors or supervisors at the district level. Comparing the amount of instructional time allocated for basic skills on your child's schedule to the time table in this chapter will help you to analyze the acceptability of his individual allotment of instructional time. Is he in the low average, average, or high average time table?

▶ **Skill #2: Use your child's instructional time schedule to determine the best time to schedule doctor's and other necessary outside appointments.**

For example, if he has more difficulty with math than any other subject, obviously you would want to try to schedule appointments during "nonmath" times of the school day.

Discussing scheduling options with your child as you review the schedule together will help him recognize the value of time, think in logical patterns, and begin to perceive time as something that can be effectively managed in one's best interest and the interests of others.

▶ **Skill #3: Schedule conferences to resolve instructional schedule deficiencies and keep written records of these meetings.**

If you discover that your child's schedule is unacceptable, there are several options. Schedule a conference with one or several of the following:

- Teacher(s)
- Principal or Assistant Principal
- Guidance Counselor
- Curriculum Specialist/Primary Specialist
- Director of Elementary Education (or equivalent position)
- Superintendent or Assistant Superintendent

Remember the interpersonal conference skills explained in Chapter 3. In most instances, it is prudent to plan conferences with the "higher-ups" only after several school level efforts have failed, primarily because they usually will ask if you have met those directly related to the issue, and, therefore, closer to the problem.

It's advisable to record the dates of the school conferences, the results of each conference, and the names and titles of those who attended. Then if it is necessary to schedule conferences with county-level administrators, you will have information easily available rather than committed to memory, a memory which may not accurately recall all details.

If your child's instructional schedule deficiencies are not satisfactorily worked out in conferencing, you may want to consider changing teachers, schools, or districts. Teacher reassignment is discussed in Chapter 4. Districts usually have strict guidelines, procedures, and policies about changing schools within the district. The district administrative offices will have the guidelines available if you wish to know the district's procedures.

▶ **Skill #4: When an instructional time deficit exists, weigh the potential harm to your child if the schedule remains unchanged against the potential gain if the schedule is changed.**

The scheduling information in this chapter needs to be used prudently, practically, and wisely. Obviously, parents cannot demand totally unique instructional time schedules for each of the approximately twenty-five children in every classroom. Twenty-five conflicting schedules would not be functional. A point of diminishing returns and haphazard inefficiency would result.

▶ **Skill #5: Determine whether or not your child's instructional schedule provides reasonable amounts of quality instructional time for achievement in those areas in which she is required to achieve.**

In other words, if your child is required to perform in math, is there appropriate quality instructional math time for her to achieve the necessary math skills? In order to determine this you need to ask these questions.

▶ **Question #1: Does your child receive quality instructional time?**

"Quality instructional time" comprises a variety of qualities and quantities, such as teacher method and planning, learning atmosphere, students' attentiveness and level of absorption, specific amount of time given to the subject and corrective teacher/student feedback, and prior learning.

We will discuss only those "quality time issues" that parents could easily observe, question, and, therefore, help to improve. The quality time factor is a separate discussion from amount (or quantity) of time scheduled. Quality has to do with the uses or misuses of the scheduled time for learning a subject and/or skill(s). Quality instructional time might best be explained by illustrating the lack of it.

Unfortunately, I have seen several teachers torture themselves and their students by "teaching" a subject when those intended to learn that subject weren't actively listening. In extreme cases students were crawling around the classroom, fighting, throwing objects, yelling, and generally ignoring the "teacher" who was standing in front of the room oblivious to the children and absorbed in his own presentation of the subject. Tragic, yes! Unbelievable, no! I've seen this repeatedly in classrooms. It's all too believable and regrettable for me.

In less severe cases (only less severe in terms of safety, still severe in terms of instructional deprivation), students sit passively staring at the one who misguidedly calls herself "teacher" while she drones on and on about a subject that is made to sound as exciting as leftover mush from seventeenth-century English orphanages.

Children subjected to these instructional methods are being deprived of their rightful educational opportunities, all or most of which are probably mentioned either directly or indirectly in the educational philosophy written by the educators at your child's school.

A CHILD'S EDUCATIONAL RIGHTS:

1. To enjoy learning new and interesting information
2. To develop critical thinking processes
3. To develop productive and satisfying relations with others through discussion skills
4. To express creativity and originality
5. To experience the joy of spending time productively
6. To experience the pleasure of learning about one's own limitations and strengths
7. To experience the pleasure of academic achievement
8. To exercise the mind with relevant, developmental, and personally enriching experiences and knowledge
9. To be assured of physical safety

10. To experience a constructive, interpersonal school relationship with the teacher(s)

I've had a difficult time appreciating why teachers abuse children by denying them these opportunities. Perhaps it's lack of energy, lack of interest, lack of concern, too many years in the profession, not enough years in the profession. Who knows? Whatever the teacher's reasons for this (one hopes) unconscious neglect, parents need not allow their children to suffer the consequences of daily subjection to unprofessional behavior.

In my recollection of my own schooling, the best teachers taught me to think, analyze, evaluate, synthesize, investigate, create, initiate, and become more independent and confident. These teachers taught me to cope creatively with my world! Yet, I've heard so many parents say that their child must learn to cope with life in the real world and, therefore, having an unacceptable teacher is just a part of learning to cope. Coping with unprofessional, unskilled, and interpersonally crippled teachers taught me little about my inner strength which would help me cope as an adult. The rationale that it is acceptable to leave a child in the classroom of a teacher who is unacceptable for that child simply because "a child needs to learn to cope with the real world," is absolutely unfounded and destructive of the child's best interests. I would compare it to the decision of an attorney that a few unacceptable jurors were all right, because the client needed, after all, to learn to deal with the real world. Educational deprivation has never been, never will be, and never should be, the behavioral tool responsible adults use to teach children to effectively cope with life's problems.

The ten educational rights of children listed above can best be ensured if we know how to prevent abuse by learning how to recognize high quality instruction. You don't need to be a professional educator to recognize sound instruction. You only need to be a positive, objective, supportive person with knowledge of a few easily observable characteristics of teaching techniques.

When you visit your child's classroom, look for these easily observable interactions between teachers and students. Of course, there are many personalities in the classroom; individual students will respond differently to the teacher. However, the overall tenor of the class should enable you to interpret the behaviors identified in the list.

TEN OBSERVABLE CHARACTERISTICS OF QUALITY INSTRUCTIONAL TIME

The Teacher	*Therefore, Your Child:*
1. Encourages questions and gives appropriate responsible feedback.	Asks questions and responds positively to correction.
2. Is enthusiastic about learning and teaching.	Has a good relationship with the teacher.
3. Recognizes and rewards student success.	Is eager to respond to teacher's direction and assistance.
4. Encourages independent behavior and self-confidence.	Has self-disciplined behavior and confidence.
5. Combines many instructional methods (lecture, hands-on activities, problem-solving, discussion, other).	Is interested in the instructional program (evidenced by attentiveness and responsiveness).
6. Stimulates the students' curiosity and promotes the joy of learning (e.g., offers verbal and physical expressions of encouragement; displays children's work/activities in classroom).	Expresses pleasure about successful academic and social achievements and new learning experiences.

TEN OBSERVABLE CHARACTERISTICS OF QUALITY INSTRUCTIONAL TIME

The Teacher	*Therefore, Your Child:*
7. Encourages values of integrity, respect for one another, honesty, thoughtfulness, and character.	Demonstrates responsible conduct toward other students.
8. Is knowledgeable of subject and establishes high standards of student achievement consistent with each student's abilities.	Acquires new academic knowledge, skills, and life-enriching experiences.
9. Encourages the initiation and communication of ideas and the evaluation of those ideas.	Enjoys creatively sharing written and oral thoughts and the analysis of those thoughts.
10. Maintains discipline for a productive, efficient, pleasant learning environment.	Is constructively involved and on-task in small groups, individual assignments, or with the teacher. Can also perform tasks without constant teacher contact.

Question #2: Is the ambience of the school and classroom contributing negatively or positively to the quality of the instructional time?

If your child is in a physically depressing, unattractive school environment, it is unlikely that this environment will encourage/promote quality instructional time. John Goodlad, former Dean of the graduate school of education at the University of California and a prominent author in the field of education, reported in "What Some Schools and Classrooms

Teach" that of the 129 elementary schools he visited throughout the United States, "only a few were architecturally pleasing." For example, "One set of three schools, elementary, middle and senior high, on a flat site was so drab, dirty, and unadorned with landscaping or color that I could only wonder about the impact on students having to spend 12 consecutive years of their lives there."

Are research studies necessary for everything we attempt to analyze? Wouldn't it be enough to ask ourselves as Child Advocate/Representatives if the school environment is stimulating, interesting, and conducive to growth and learning? Could we ourselves spend five hours a day every day in that facility and perform to our full potential?

Question # 3: Is there time that is obviously, unreasonably misspent?

Now we have grabbed a tiger by the tail! Can we agree about the appropriate use of instructional time? The professional teachers of the arts want more time; the reading teachers want more time; the social science, math, health, and physical education teachers want more time. Each can present a philosophically sound argument for scheduling more curriculum time for his particular area of expertise. As a professional, I, of course, am saddled with my own biases. The arts, in my estimation, are at least of equal, if not of more, importance to humankind than the academic "basics." Integrity, character, honesty, and other worthwhile values can be learned and expressed through the arts.

Physical education is another positive bias of mine. I think it is unfortunate that usually only team sports such as soccer, volleyball, football, basketball, track, and baseball are emphasized. Large-group or team sports activities serve many valuable purposes, but how many of us can actually actively use these sports for "lifelong" exercise and recreation? Golf, tennis, swimming, and badminton are all sports which could be more practically used in a "lifelong" plan of exercise and physical pleasure, but most U.S. elementary schools do not encourage or provide for these sports in their physical education (PE) programs. Cost is a factor, but tradition, habit, and difficulty of change probably are the main reasons behind the perpetuation of programs which I consider to be misusing a great deal of the instructional time allocated for PE.

Certainly parents who want to produce a great football star would be likely to disagree with my definition of the appropriate use of PE time. This illustrates why reasonable determination of misspent instructional time is a difficult task. If you do not intend to address the entire "curriculum issue," may I suggest that you consider the question of misspent time only as it relates to quality instructional issues pertaining to your child.

The following story about Tommy clearly illustrates misspent instructional time. Tommy was an attractive, curious, gifted child in third grade. He attended the school's gifted program for two hours a week, which was the normal schedule for all children in the program. During the other schoolday hours he was in the regular classroom. His teacher was wonderfully talented when working with remedial students and average-ability children. But Tommy didn't fall into either category, and the teacher subsequently was frustrated.

Tommy read on the sixth grade level and functioned on the eighth grade level in math. Even with Tommy placed in the highest grade-level instructional groups, the teacher still didn't meet his academic needs or interests, nor challenge his potential. He began third grade by spending most of his day completing the class assignments quickly and proudly submitting them to the teacher, who in turn would hand him more paperwork to "keep him busy." It didn't take long before Tommy figured out that the sooner he completed his assignments, the more work he was given. He began to take his time completing the original assignments. Then he became careless and not interested. By the end of third grade he no longer proudly completed anything. His products were unacceptable by third grade standards and definitely so by "gifted" standards. The teacher told the parents that she was very disappointed with Tommy's progress, particularly because he had so much potential. He was, also, becoming a disruptive element in the classroom.

Tommy's time was misspent. He should not have been penalized because of his intellectual level or because others in the class "needed the teacher more," as his teacher often said. There are so many interesting, challenging materials available which could have helped Tommy spend each school day productively and happily. Additional paperwork was only one of many options open to the teacher.

Often these materials already exist within the school facility or in nearby schools. If money is needed to purchase material, the PTA/PTO in schools are usually eager to support worthwhile causes for a curriculum that is well-balanced for all children.

Tommy could have been challenged with a new language, computer skills, scientific research and so much more. His teacher needed help exploring resources and possible educational program options. A Curriculum Specialist, the "gifted program" teacher, an administrator, a classroom teacher, or a parent who had developed EP-A/R skills could have devised a curriculum that permitted the teacher ample time for all of her students while providing an educationally-enriching program for Tommy.

Though, of course, the teacher was at fault, it was also critical to Tommy's third grade problems that his parents failed to detect this misspent instructional time before he developed unacceptable behavior patterns which then became difficult to correct.

There may also be misspent time in supplementary programs outside of the regular classrooms and in the special student service programs. This was discussed in Chapter 6.

▶ **Skill # 6: Use the checklist of observable characteristics of quality instructional time (Form D, page 199) to help you make an objective analysis of your child's daily program.**
Review the list before visiting the classroom, and record your reactions as soon as possible after your visit. At the same time you may also wish to use Form A (page 185) for determining teacher acceptability. You may discover that your child's program is excellent, or at least satisfactory. Indeed, your particular child may just need "extra" quality time to absorb certain material or to learn new skills. Providing additional time for learning has often helped children overcome academic hurdles.

However, if there clearly is a lack of quality instructional time, refer to Chapter 4, When the Teacher Is the Problem. It could help you successfully have your child assigned to a new teacher.

SUMMARY

ITM GOAL: TO REVIEW THE APPROPRIATENESS OF AMOUNTS OF TIME SCHEDULED FOR EACH SUBJECT AREA FOR YOUR CHILD AND TO DETERMINE THE QUALITY OF THAT SCHEDULED INSTRUCTIONAL TIME IN ORDER TO ASSURE THAT YOUR CHILD HAS THE BEST POSSIBLE OPPORTUNITY TO MASTER THE REQUIRED CURRICULUM.

ITM Secrets

Secret # 1: Your child may or may not be receiving enough quality instructional time to master the required curriculum.

Secret # 2: Often the instructional time schedule of individual teachers varies drastically within the same school and same grade level. Therefore some children receive much less instructional time than others to achieve the same academic requirements.

Secret #3: Some teachers do not schedule instructional time following required state and district guidelines.

Secret #4: Scheduled instructional time is often abused because of the teacher's misuse of that time.

Secret #5: The time your child spends "successfully engaged" may be minimal.

Secret #6: If the classroom teacher does not have a well-outlined daily and weekly schedule, no matter what the reason given you, your child's time is being wasted.

ITM Skills

Skill #1: Obtain a written schedule of your child's instructional school day, including noninstructional activities such as lunch, to help you monitor and analyze the use of time.

Skill #2: Use the written schedule to determine the best times to schedule appointments that require your child to be away from school.

Skill #3: Schedule appointments with school personnel in order to resolve your child's instructional schedule deficiencies. Maintain a written record of every conference including the purpose, the results, who attended, the dates and places.

Skill #4: Weigh the potential harm to your child if the schedule remains unchanged against the potential gain if the schedule is changed.

Skill #5: Determine if your child is receiving quality instruction time, if the ambience in the school and classroom is good, and if there is time obviously misspent.

Skill #6: Prior to visiting the classroom, review the checklist of ten observable characteristics of quality instructional time provided in Form D (on page 199). Record your reactions after leaving the classroom. You may also choose to use Form A (page 185) on teacher acceptability.

MOVING FORWARD . . .

The next chapter, Chapter 8, contains the forms that have been referred to as you read the preceeding chapters. While reading those chapters, it may have been awkward to turn several pages ahead to Chapter 8, but several forms pertain to more than one chapter or skill and to prevent copying the same form several times it was more efficient to place them together in one chapter. In addition, I wanted to make using these forms convenient for you during your child's elementary school years. Therefore, it seemed best to package them in one chapter than to scatter them throughout the book. I hope you find them helpful tools for collecting and organizing your perceptions about your child's school(s) and teacher(s).

8
Organize Your Perceptions: Forms to Guide You

As I write this chapter, a phantom administrator sits on one shoulder, the custodian of the Pandora's box I may be opening, exposing my colleagues to increased harassment from the gargoyles. On the other shoulder sits the spirit of a child imploring me to overcome my anxieties over the obscene and destructive nature of these creatures, anxieties which, if I heeded them, could prevent me from providing needed information about analyzing teacher, curriculum, and facility acceptability.

The gargoyles are those few parents who intentionally victimize teachers and administrators for malicious purposes with no constructive goals. Their "I'll get the establishment" attitudes fester and spew out toward the school system. Some have college educations, impressive community responsibilities, and social status; others have little education, few or no community and job responsibilities, and low social standing. Regardless, both strains of gargoyles lack a sense of propriety, tend to ventilate hostile-aggressive vulgarities without consideration of consequences, and inject their poisonous venom into relationships.

When I respond to the question "What is the title of your

book?" the gargoyles' eyes literally gleam with the prospect of new ammunition because they assume that something or someone is being criticized. "Ah," they say, "*Secrets Parents Should Know About Public Elementary Schools*. What a great idea!" Romans feeding Christians to lions could have expressed no more demonic, sadistic delight than do these gargoyles at the delicious thought of learning unexpurgated secrets about the system to use against the system. Their needs to feel superior and to exert power, the dissonance they create, the mistrust they sew, their unending ill-considered attempts to institute radical innovation, and their general lack of integrity are a few of the traits by which they blatently advertise their malevolent presence.

They are a menace to themselves, to the school system, and, more tragically, to their children.

I am repelled when I talk with them, but I shudder when I consider their potential abuses of the information in this chapter. Dare I listen to the spirit of the child or should I allow myself to be seduced by the phantom? It would be far easier to heed the entreaties of the phantom administrator to suppress all information that gargoyles could distort for self-serving and destructive purposes than it would be to release information and encourage the use of it in the best interests of our children. I seriously considered foregoing this chapter, but providing you with the criteria by which you can make decisions based upon well-supported data and informing you of reasonable expectations of teacher performance and classroom dynamics was important to the continuity of this book. Most of the administrators and teachers with whom I've worked have learned to cope with the gargoyles. These monsters make their work less tolerable, but they can be controlled. Their obvious hostility usually diffuses their influence. With this in mind, I resolved my dilemma in favor of the spirit of the child, who convinced me to have faith in the many well-intentioned parents who want harmony. They wish no one ill; they care for their children and desire only that the schools are happy and productive places for all. This chapter is not explosive or shocking. As a matter of fact, it is one of the few chapters in which there are no secrets. As you read each question on the forms, you will experience little surprise, even though without professional training you might not have thought to ask all of them. You'll probably feel a comfortable, flowing sense of, "Of course, these are practical questions I should consider as I determine whether the teacher, curriculum, and facility are suitable for my child."

Used with reason and sensitivity, these forms have only inherently constructive potential. It's only my knowledge that they will be misused by a few that causes me concern. I have nightmares of a gargoyle reading this chapter and waving his neat collection of forms under the nose of an unsuspecting administrator and demanding teacher dismissals and radical building renovation.

If all this gargoyle business seems to you slightly overdone and a bit paranoid, keep in mind that teachers and school administrators work with the same general public that many of you do. In my experience, 95 percent of parents are supportive and offer constructive criticism. The other 5 percent are the gargoyles, a group that consistently complains and whose complaints are often unreasonable and hostile, reflecting more the nature of the complainer than the problem. Veteran educators are well acquainted with the gargoyles, enemies of creative, constructive problem-solving. I wish to offer them no aid or comfort.

LET'S BE CLEAR ABOUT WHAT THESE FORMS CAN AND CANNOT DO!

First, and most important, *these forms can help you organize your own perceptions* by providing instruments for recording specific observations and grouping them visually. The information collected will reflect your general impressions about the "acceptability" of teacher, curriculum, and facility.

Second, *they present in question form "reasonable expecta-tions"* generally used by the profession to evaluate itself and its facilities. It makes sense to know and to use these stan-dards for the purpose of focusing your impressions to help you arrive at critical EP-A/R decisions.

The forms *cannot provide evidence* (except about physical facilities). Evidence is derived from *facts*. When you have filled in every blank, you will have an organized list of your own *observations*, at best honestly but subjectively deter-mined. These organized observations can merely lead you to collective impressions from which you will make decisions.

They cannot be used to determine teacher competency or curriculum adequacy. Skilled administrators with years of ex-perience approach teacher evaluation with caution. They tend to develop sensitivities that help them mentally balance a "best foot forward" teacher performance with the tension and anxiety that might accompany the stressful experience of evaluation. They learn to guard against their subjectivity, recognizing that into every human encounter we carry our-selves—our backgrounds, our personalities, our prejudices, our values, and our bodies. We have no other means of ex-periencing life. Even an evaluation by a qualified professional that reflected a "poor" job performance would call for more thorough investigation and would not be conclusive evidence affecting future employment.

This book does not suggest that you shoulder the awesome burden of evaluating a teacher, but rather encourages you *to accept responsibility for ensuring that your child is suitably placed.* In a spirit of fairness and integrity, dare to form im-pressions and act upon them. If you fear that your observa-tions may lead you to take a position that could do someone damage, that's good. It means you're not a gargoyle. If your observations lead you to highly positive impressions, tell peo-ple. They'll appreciate knowing. Genuine compliments are priceless. If your conclusions tend to be critical, treat them like a "hot potato."

THE HOT POTATO POLICY: First, cool down a bit. Don't make any decision prodded by heated emotions. Treat the issues gently; let the steam escape. Second, decide how best to approach the problem(s). Should you take tiny little bites to resolve them or a heaping forkful? Finally, armed with your utensils—EP-A/R skills—*dig in!*

SUGGESTION: You may want to consider making copies of these forms on which to check your responses or to record notes. If you have several children or just a single child, you may find that you will want to use the forms over and over again throughout several school years, and these copies may be most helpful.

▷ Form A: Is the teacher acceptable for my child?

Can we be absolutely certain that every checkmark we make on this form is a legitimate, clear interpretation of the classroom situation? No, of course not. We strive for objectivity, but at best, we are humans—end of argument.

The items listed on this form are based upon three sources: the generally accepted minimal standards of performance of the education profession, Florida Teacher Competency concepts and ideas, and the Florida State Board of Education Rules entitled "Standards of Competent Professional Performance." This form is not an evaluation or observation instrument for use to determine teacher competence or job performance. It is strictly intended to aid parents in their pursuit of excellence as Educational Planners and to help them determine whether or not the teacher is an "acceptable" instructor *for their child.* To do that, all you need to do is give your honest impressions to each item. The ultimate decision—whether or not to leave your child in the present teacher's classroom—will emerge as you observe your child in class, respond to the items, and analyze the data you'll collect. Follow the guidelines carefully. They are critical to the successful use of this form.

Guidelines for Using the Teacher-Acceptability Form

1. Always make an appointment with the teacher(s) in advance of your visit to the classroom. The visit should last at least an hour during prime instructional time (PIT) and should take place during a typical school day (not during school-picture day, for example).

2. When you visit, maintain the demeanor suggested in the Parent Conference Profile in Chapter 3, page 61.

3. *Do not under any circumstances take this form with you when you visit the classroom.* Taking this form and checking off items while you're visiting would be gargoyle behavior and extremely inappropriate interpersonally.

4. Review the form a few times before visiting the classroom. Familiarize yourself with every item and prepare to analyze specifics. (This is much easier than it may sound.)

5. Check each of the items as soon as possible after leaving the school premises; otherwise you may forget important factors.

6. Use the data you collected prudently. Take action if the "seldoms" outweigh (not necessarily outnumber) the "usuallys" and if your child would be at a disadvantage spending an entire school year in that classroom. Remember the Hot Potato Policy. Even the best of teachers may have a "seldom," but the best of teachers will not have many "seldoms" unless your judgement was grossly incorrect. (Eagles have buzzard days just as parents have gargoyle days when they are not usually gargoyle variety.)

7. Since these checks will represent your impressions, they are not necessarily limited to the time span of the visit alone. Many of the items include the words "your child." It would be literally impossible within the context of a full classroom for the teacher to interact with any one child in all of these ways in one hour. However, your child may have reported on several occasions that she was complimented or publicly crit-

icized or didn't have enough time to finish assigned work. If you have any reasonably derived impressions from sources other than your visit, include them on your form with notes to yourself explaining the details.

FORM # A
IS THE TEACHER ACCEPTABLE FOR MY CHILD?

Classroom Visit: School _____

Date: _____ **Time:** _____ **Grade:** _____

Teacher: _____

Child: _____

Parent: _____

Instruction: _____

(Subjects taught during visit)

CRITERIA FOR ACCEPTABILITY

	(check responses)	
I. CLASSROOM MANAGEMENT	*Usually*	*Seldom*
1. The room is orderly considering the limitations of the existing facility and your child's academic and emotional needs.		
2. The necessary materials for each task are easily and efficiently distributed in an orderly manner, causing little or no classroom disruption.		
3. Your child has the materials required to complete assigned tasks (for example: texts, equipment, supplies).		
4. Daily routines that do not have an instructional focus are effectively organized to avoid wasting prime instructional time (for example: roll call, lunch ticket distribution, preparing to go out to recess).		

	(check responses)	
	Usually	*Seldom*
5. The students are busy with assigned tasks giving your child ample opportunity to complete tasks to the best of his ability.		
6. If a disturbance occurs, the teacher handles the misconduct quickly and with minimal loss of PIT. (For example: Is an inordinate amount of time spent upon a minor infraction, and/or does the disturbance cause all students to lose valuable instructional time?)		
7. The teacher appropriately circulates in the classroom and assists children with their assignments.		
8. When the teacher works with a small number of students, are the other students able to successfully complete tasks without constant teacher-pupil interaction?		
9. The teacher's voice quality is acceptable (he avoids loud-grating, high-pitched monotone and inaudible voice distortions).		
10. The teacher's speech is clear and understandable.		
11. The learning atmosphere is positive, interesting, and stimulating for your child.		
12. Discipline is maintained sufficiently for your child to have the opportunity to enjoy the benefits of a productive learning atmosphere.		

II. STUDENT-TEACHER RELATIONSHIPS	*Usually*	*Seldom*
1. The teacher praises and encourages your child.		
2. The teacher offers only constructive, nonjudgmental criticism (she does not intentionally make comments which embarrass your child).		
3. The teacher demonstrates an overall regard for children as individuals with feelings, rights, responsibilities, and strengths.		
4. The teacher is alert to the physical and emotional needs of children.		
5. The teacher calmly states reasonable consequences for misconduct and follows through with consequences whenever necessary.		
6. Motivational factors are easily apparent. The classroom has visible signs of the teacher's efforts to motivate your child (for example: a display of students' work/achievements).		
7. The teacher encourages the development of your child's potential.		
III. INSTRUCTIONAL PROGRAM REVIEW		
1. The teacher uses an appropriate variety of activities consistent with your child's abilities. (For example: Does the teacher offer assignments other than daily paperwork tasks? Does the level of the tasks assigned cause your child to have expectations of failure or success?)		
2. The teacher encourages questions from children.		

	Usually	Seldom
3. The teacher asks questions of children which require reasoning, analysis, and factual responses. (For example: Does the teacher ask questions that require more than yes or no answers?)		
4. The teacher's instructional methods are stimulating and interesting. He makes whatever subject is being taught as interesting as possible and identifies the relevance of the material to the students; his enthusiasm is evident.		
5. Continuity of the instructional program is clear. The teacher opens and closes lessons with a brief summary of what was learned yesterday, what was learned today, and what will be learned tomorrow.		
6. Your child is given sufficient directions to enable her to understand assignments.		
7. Your child is able to obtain a satisfactory measure of success commensurate with her ability. Genuine effort is made to meet the instructional needs of your child.		
8. The teacher uses multilevel classroom materials and makes assignments appropriate to your child's abilities. (For example: Some children in first grade may need second-grade-level materials; others may need kindergarten instructional material.)		

	Usually	*Seldom*
9. Long- and short-range objectives are planned, and the teacher is striving to help your child achieve those objectives. (Discuss these objectives with the teacher during a conference.)		

OTHER: (Comments; facts you may need to remember for future reference.)

▷ **Forms B and C: My child's daily instructional schedule.**

In Chapter 7, Skill #1, I recommended that all parents at the beginning of every school year routinely obtain a written schedule of their child's complete school day. Either of these two optional Instructional Time Management forms will provide a concrete picture of the way your child's instructional time is allocated. Use whichever one you prefer, or design a form of your own. The teacher might also have one that will serve the purpose. Two samples of completed forms are provided so you can familiarize yourself with the objective prior to using one of the ITM forms or to designing a form of your own. Remember, you are not being unreasonable or rigid in expecting the teacher to account for all of the time your child is at school. That is a generally accepted part of his responsibility.

FORM # B

DAILY SCHEDULE (EXAMPLE ONLY)

School: Cheerful Elementary   Child: John Goodman

Parent(s): Ms. Working Mother   Grade: 1   Room: 103

Teacher: Mr. Tops   Year: 1986

TIME	MONDAY	TIME	TUESDAY	TIME	WEDNESDAY	TIME	THURSDAY	TIME	FRIDAY
9:00–11:30	Language Arts	9:00–11:30	Language Arts	9:00–11:30	Language Arts	9:00–11:30	Language Arts	9:00–11:30	Language Arts
11:30–12:00	Lunch	11:30–12:00	Lunch	11:30–12:00	Lunch	11:30–12:00	Lunch	11:30–12:00	Lunch
12:00–12:30	Art	12:00–1:00	Math	12:00–12:30	Music	12:00–1:00	Math	12:00–12:30	Library
12:30–1:00	Math			12:30–1:00	Math			12:30–1:00	Math
1:00–1:30	SLD	1:00–1:30	SLD	1:00–1:30	SLD	1:00–1:30	SLD	1:00–1:30	SLD
1:30–2:00	Physical Education	1:30–2:00	Recess	1:30–2:00	Physical Education	1:30–2:00	Recess	1:30–2:00	Recess
2:00–2:30	Math	2:00–2:45	Science	2:00–2:30	Math	2:00–2:45	Social Studies	2:00–2:30	Math
2:30–2:45	Health			2:30–2:45	Career Ed or Health			2:30–2:45	Enrichment
2:45–3:00	Dismissal	2:45–3:00	Dismissal	2:45–3:00	Dismissal	2:45–3:00	Dismissal	2:45–3:00	Dismissal

NOTE: Language Arts for elementary school should include at least spelling, handwriting, phonics, listening skills, reading (or readiness), English, oral and written expression.

FORM # B
DAILY SCHEDULE (EXAMPLE ONLY)

School: _____

Parent(s): _____

Teacher: _____

Child: _____

Grade: _____

Year: _____

Room: _____

Time	Monday	Time	Tuesday	Time	Wednesday	Time	Thursday	Time	Friday

FORM # c
DAILY SCHEDULE (EXAMPLE ONLY)

School: Happy Elementary   **Grade:** 3

Child: Mary Sunshine   **Teacher:** Ms. Pleasant   **Year:** 1985

Parent: Mr. & Mrs. Concerned   **Room:** 36

Time of Day	Monday	Tuesday	Wednesday	Thursday	Friday
8:00	8:00–10:30 Language Arts	8:00–10:30 Language Arts	8:00–8:30 Language Arts	8:00–8:30 Language Arts	8:00–10:30 Language Arts
8:30			8:30–9:00 Music	8:30–9:00 Art	
9:00					
9:30	Language Arts	Language Arts	9:00–10:00 Language Arts	9:00–10:00 Language Arts	Language Arts
10:00					
10:30	Language Arts	Language Arts	Language Arts	Language Arts	Language Arts
11:00	10:30–11:30 Math	10:30–11:30 Math	10:30–11:30 Math	10:30–11:30 Math	10:30–11:30 Math

	Day 1	Day 2	Day 3	Day 4	Day 5
11:30	Math	Math	Math	Math	Math
	11:30–12:00 ECIA–Ch. I. Reading	11:30–12:00 ECIA–Ch. I. Reading	11:30–12:00 ECIA–Ch. I. Reading	11:30–12:00 ECIA–Ch. I. Reading	11:30–12:00 ECIA–Ch. I. Reading
12:00	12:00–12:30 Lunch	12:00–12:30 Lunch	12:00–12:30 Lunch	12:00–12:30 Lunch	12:00–12:30 Lunch
12:30	12:30–1:00 Social Studies	12:30–1:00 Social Studies	12:30–1:00 Science	12:30–1:00 Science	12:30–1:00 Library
1:00	1:00–1:45 Physical Education	1:00–1:45 Physical Education	1:00–1:45 Recess	1:00–1:45 Recess	1:00–1:45 Recess
1:30	1:45–2:15 Health	1:45–2:15 Health	1:45–2:15 Language Arts	1:45–2:15 Language Arts	1:45–2:15 Enrichment
2:00				2:15—Dismissal Preparation 2:30—Dismissal	
2:30				DAY CARE PICK-UP AT 2:40	
3:00					

NOTE: Language Arts in elementary school should include at least spelling, handwriting, phonics, listening skills, reading (or readiness), English, oral and written expression.

FORM # C
DAILY SCHEDULE (EXAMPLE ONLY)

School: _____ Grade: _____ Year: _____
Child: _____ Teacher: _____
Parent: _____ Room: _____

Time of Day	Monday	Tuesday	Wednesday	Thursday	Friday
8:00					
8:30					
9:00					
9:30					
10:00					
10:30					
11:00					

11:30 ——

12:00

12:30 ——

1:00

1:30 ——

2:00

2:30 ——

3:00

3:30 ——

Guidelines for Using Instructional Time Management Forms

1. Schedule a conference with the teacher(s) (I suggest you do this no later than the first few weeks of school) to discuss the ITM form you have selected and request that the teacher either help you complete the schedule or that he complete it for you. Explain that you like to be aware of your child's educational program and realize how important it is that your child have sufficient time to learn that which is expected.

2. After the schedule has been completed, review it to see if the instructional-time allotments are appropriate. For example:

a. Find out the specific amounts of time your school district and state mandate or recommend for each subject area.

b. Compare your child's reading and math basic-skills-time allocations with those given in the table on page 166.

c. Is your child below grade level in a subject and receiving a minimal amount of instructional time in that subject? Is each time allocation sufficient to help your child progress satisfactorily?

d. Is your child assigned to so many programs outside of the regular classroom that she receives only fragmented instruction in the regular classroom and is still expected to accomplish the same tasks as those students who receive less fragmented instruction? Can your child academically achieve with this schedule?

3. If you have concerns about the amount of instructional time for any subject, you may wish to schedule a conference with the principal, assistant principal, teacher(s), curriculum specialist, primary specialist, or other appropriate personnel. Ask questions and take necessary action, which may include several conferences with school and district-level educators,

until you're satisfied that your child is receiving at least the time allocations for each subject that are recommended or required by the district and state.

4. Review Chapter 7 if you are unclear about the immense value of these ITM forms to your child. A few minutes of your time taken to complete one ITM form at the beginning of each school year can add immeasurably to your child's education.

▷ **Form D: Ten observable characteristics of quality instructional time, or what parents should hope to find!**

The next logical step after ensuring that appropriate amounts of instructional time are allocated is to review the quality of the scheduled time. The checklist of observable characteristics of quality instructional time is designed to heighten your awareness of desirable classroom dynamics. It is advisable to examine the quality of instructional services early on in the school year. The teacher-student relationship may enhance or detract from the effectiveness of the curriculum, thereby affecting the quality of instruction and student performance.

Guidelines for Using the Quality-of-Instructional-Time Form

1. Review the form before visiting the classroom.

2. *Do not take the form with you when you visit.*

3. Keep a positive attitude when visiting, and try to be objective.

4. Respond to the items on the checklist as soon as possible after leaving the school premises.

5. Check your responses and take action to understand the absence of the behavior when you could not check "yes."

6. This form is for parental use as a means of collecting data for effective educational planning. It is not suggested as a professional instrument for total curriculum analysis.

7. If you check "yes" to an item in the teacher's column and "no" to the same item in your child's column, then perhaps that could mean that the quality of the program is at least satisfactory and that your child needs attention from you or appropriate others who may help remedy the difficulty.

8. The *only* time that I would recommend taking this form with you to a teacher conference is when you are honestly able to check every item in the teacher's column "yes" and your child has a few "no" checks that you would like to discuss with the teacher, who may be able to help.

FORM # D
TEN OBSERVABLE CHARACTERISTICS OF QUALITY
INSTRUCTIONAL TIME or WHAT PARENTS SHOULD HOPE TO
FIND!

(check responses)				(check responses)	
Yes	*No*	THE TEACHER:	THEREFORE, YOUR CHILD:	*Yes*	*No*
		1. Encourages questions and gives appropriate responsive feedback.	Asks questions and responds positively to correction.		
		2. Is enthusiastic about learning and teaching.	Has a good relationship with the teacher.		
		3. Recognizes and rewards student success.	Is eager to respond to teacher's direction and assistance.		
		4. Encourages independent behavior and self-confidence.	Has self-disciplined behavior and confidence.		

Yes	No	THE TEACHER:	THEREFORE, YOUR CHILD:	Yes	No
		5. Combines many instructional methods (lecture, hands-on activities, problem-solving, discussion, other).	Is interested in the instructional program (evidenced by attentiveness and responsiveness).		
		6. Stimulates the students' curiosity and promotes the joy of learning (e.g., offers verbal and physical expressions of encouragement; displays children's work/activities in classroom).	Expresses pleasure about successful academic and social achievements and new learning experiences.		
		7. Encourages values of integrity, respect for one another, honesty, thoughtfulness, and character.	Demonstrates responsible conduct toward other students.		
		8. Is knowledgeable of subject and establishes high standards of achievement consistent with each student's abilities	Acquires new academic knowledge, skills, and life-enriching experiences.		
		9. Encourages the initiation and communication of ideas and the evaluation of those ideas.	Enjoys creatively sharing written and oral thoughts and the analysis of those thoughts.		

(check responses) Yes No (check responses) Yes No

| *(check responses)* | | | | *(check responses)* | |
Yes	No	THE TEACHER:	THEREFORE, YOUR CHILD:	Yes	No
		10. Maintains discipline for a productive, efficient, pleasant learning environment.	Is constructively involved and on-task in small groups, individual assignments, or with the teachers. Can also perform tasks without constant teacher contact.		

▷ **Form E: Is this a good school for my child?**

In his 1983 *Clearing House* article "Quality Control in Education," Dr. Bernard Massee defines "effective schools" in a way which I believe would represent the consensus of professional educators. He states,

> Effective schools are characterized as schools where the principal exercises strong leadership, where there is evidence of high expectations for staff and students, where a climate conducive to learning prevails, where a strong academic focus and an emphasis on basic skills pervades the school, and where a conscious effort is made to increase the time available for learning.

Can a superior curriculum exist in an ineffective school? *No!* A school's effectiveness may be judged directly as it relates to student achievement.

The definition of a quality curriculum is a continual source of contention among educators and parents. We will never agree completely upon a single curriculum design and philosophy for all public elementary schools, as well we shouldn't. Communities' needs and values vary and the curriculum should respond to those it serves. There are, however, some very basic minimal determinants of a quality curriculum. These determinants, which I will call "guides," may be used by parents as a rough measure of their child's curriculum. If your child is currently attending a public school this form will help you determine whether or not you wish your child to remain in that school.

If you are moving to a new locale, you may wish to visit a few schools before deciding upon a definite place of residence since that will usually determine which public school your child must attend. Therefore, this form may also help you determine whether or not you wish to enroll your child in a particular school.

Guidelines for Using the School-Effectiveness Form

1. Make an appointment with the school administration before your visit. Ask to speak to someone who has a few minutes to give you a tour of the school and explain your reason for visiting. And (if school is in session), ask if it would be possible to visit several classrooms. If so, it is usually best to remain in the classrooms for only a few minutes and make every effort not to interrupt instruction.

2. Review the form before your visit.

3. *Do not take the form with you when you visit.*

4. Respond to the items on the form as soon as possible after your visit.

5. As you respond to the items on the checklist, you will notice that a few items seem to apply only to a situation of current enrollment and not to a "new school." On these items simply ask yourself if, from your observations of the new school, you would be likely to check yes. For example, see items #8, #11, and #12.

FORM # E

IS THIS A GOOD SCHOOL FOR MY CHILD?

Elementary School: _____ Grade(s): _____

Principal: _____ Date(s): _____

QUALITY CRITERIA	*(check responses)* Yes	No
1. The general administrator-student, teacher-student atmosphere is conducive to your child's learning.		
2. The general student-student school atmosphere is conducive to your child's learning.		
3. There is a reasonable instructional time period given to every subject area in which your child is expected to achieve. (NOTE: There should be opportunities for your child to learn to read well, to communicate orally and in writing, to develop skill in mathematics, and to develop an understanding of social and scientific worlds of knowledge.)		
4. Teacher morale appears good and results in good student morale. (NOTE: Children seem to enjoy being at school.)		
5. The overall climate of the school is conducive to a healthy, constructive learning environment for your child.		
6. The overall classroom climate is conducive to your child's learning (observe class size, racial balance, discipline, evidence of effort to motivate students, other).		
7. The school population's standardized test results indicate that they compare well with other state and national student populations. (NOTE: The annual school and district report(s) to parents should discuss these test results).		
8. The teacher acceptably addresses your child's educational, social, and emotional needs within the context of the school situation.		
9. Appropriate texts, equipment, and supplies are provided.		
10. The physical facility is safe, efficient, well-maintained, and pleasant. It effectively supports regular and/or special education classes for your child.		
11. The curriculum addresses the intellectual, social, emotional, and physical needs of your child. (NOTE: This includes Exceptional Child Education needs.)		

		(check responses)	
		Yes	*No*
12.	Your child receives a "fair" portion of individualized attention for his ability.		
13.	The teachers instructing your child are certificated by the state.		
14.	Learning experiences beyond the classroom and the school facility are provided (for example, field trips).		
15.	Other: (Comments; facts you may need to remember for future references).		

▷ **Form F: Does my child need a new classroom environment?**

In Chapter 4, environmental factors unrelated to the teacher were discussed as viable reasons to request another classroom assignment for your child. Several examples of creative EP-A/R management were given. Remember that having a child withdrawn from one class and reassigned to another can be embarrassing and threatening to teachers. Therefore, if environmental factors which exclude the teacher can be identified as legitimate reasons for reassignment, then the reassignment is more likely to occur and with less interpersonal friction for yourself and your child. The intent of this form is:

• To provide an objective list of classroom environmental considerations.

• To serve as a basis for discussion in a conference requesting a new assignment (or improvements in the present classroom)

Guidelines For Using the Classroom-Environment Form

1. Observe the physical facility according to the items listed on the form. Add other issues that may concern you.

2. Your primary goal is to determine first if the environment is safe and second if it is conducive to learning.

3. Consider your child's health as it relates to the facility.

4. When there are adverse situations affecting your child, you may decide to discuss them with the principal.

5. Should you identify something that places your child or others in immediate physical danger, report it immediately to the principal.

6. This form and the data collected may be used during a conference with appropriate school personnel.

7. If your child's classroom could adversely affect his health or safety or his academic, social, or emotional development, and another classroom is likely to positively affect development and provide safety, then you have a good case for requesting a change in classroom assignment.

FORM # F
DOES MY CHILD NEED A NEW CLASSROOM ENVIRONMENT?

(Check all items that apply to your child's classroom(s):)

Yes	No	Does your child's school have:
		1. Adequate heat, air, and ventilation?
		2. Adequate bathroom facilities?
		3. Water fountains?
		4. Windows providing natural light?
		5. Distracting noise? (for example, from busy highway)? Carpets?
		6. Exceptional Child Programs, that if attended by your child, are a reasonable distance from your child's regular classroom?
		7. An ECIA Chapter I program, that if attended by your child, is a reasonable distance from your child's regular classroom?
		8. Adequate lighting?
		9. Portable classrooms that have covered walkways to the main building? (Note: Some schools are fortunate enough not to have portable classroom facilities.)

(Check all items that apply to your child's classroom(s):)

Yes	No	Does your child's school have:
		10. Adequate facilities provided for those with physical handi-caps?
		11. Desks and/or tables that are arranged in a logical pattern that facilitates a good, safe traffic flow within the classroom(s)?
		12. Furniture that is arranged to accommodate small- and large-group instruction?
		13. A size of the furniture appropriate to the size of your child?
		14. Colors which are conducive to learning?
		15. Adequate equipment and materials available for instruction and organized within the classroom(s)?
		16. An open-space facility where many teachers and children are in one large classroom?
		17. Self-contained (traditional) classrooms? (One teacher to one room)?
		18. Clean and well-maintained classrooms?
		19. For a child with serious or chronic health problems: class-room(s) within a reasonable distance from the clinic and/or office?
		20. Other:

▷ **Form G: The people at school are special to our family.**
This form serves several purposes. First and foremost, it gives your family another opportunity to teach your son or daughter to respect and show appreciation for those special people at school who work so hard to provide a quality education for him or her. Two ways that the family can express appreciation are *to recognize* special events of a personal and a school nature and *to create* special events honoring those who have been extraordinarily caring for your child.

A second purpose of this form is to have a list of all those who work with your child and their room numbers.

Genuine efforts to express support and caring enhance faculty morale and, therefore, are directly beneficial to all the children. Parents make a big difference in faculty morale. For example, a group of parents decided to honor a very special, outstandingly skilled first grade teacher. They made a treasure chest filled with little prizes for her class, and they crowned her teacher of the week! She was thrilled and her students enjoyed the treats. Everyone profited! Any adult who teaches twenty to thirty young children every day of the work week needs a pat on the back once in a while. A little appreciation goes a long way.

Offered here are only a few suggestions and one means of collecting information about special events and people at school. Be creative! Your family can surely think of many more ways to express support and caring for those who play such important roles in your child's life. Parents who practice this craft tend to rear children who look for things to praise in others. Who knows, if we really do a good job of setting this example, we might one day hear its echo, "Thanks Mom and Dad."

Guidelines for Using the School-Personnel-Appreciation Form

1. In a conference with the teacher or principal explain the reasons for wanting this information.

2. Space is left under each general category of employment for you to write the names of those whom you wish to recognize. You may not need to fill in names under each category because some don't affect your child.

3. If you collect information, use it. Post it in a central location where everyone in the family can be a part of remembering to appreciate people at school.

4. "Special occasions" can be birthdays, baby showers, weddings, workdays, record days, or teacher-of-the-week awards. If the teacher chooses not to name an occasion that is special to her, you may decide to honor her in a way your family creatively chooses.

FORM # G

THE PEOPLE AT SCHOOL ARE SPECIAL TO OUR FAMILY

School: _____

Child: _____ **Parent:** _____

Teacher: _____ **Grade:** _____ **Date:** _____

PERSONNEL	SPECIAL OCCASIONS	ROOM NUMBERS
OFFICE STAFF:		
CLASSROOM TEACHER(S) (Includes physical education)		
HUMANITIES PROGRAM TEACHERS (Music, Art, Library)		
EXCEPTIONAL CHILD EDUCATION TEACHERS		
FEDERAL PROGRAM TEACHER(S)		
CAFETERIA STAFF		
CUSTODIAL STAFF		
OTHER		

9

Letters to and from Terry: Musings of the Author—an Educator, a Parent

In the first eight chapters, I've shared system secrets and offered concrete suggestions to help cope with the system. Yet, just as a painter, with brushes still wet, steps away from her canvas, surveys it, and feels it call to her to add a few final touches, so I can't put my pen down until I share something more.

In this chapter, I've painted a few last touches. I've written letters to children who made permanent impressions upon my life and for whom I will always care. I've written a letter to my colleagues who made teaching a pleasure and for whom I will always care. I've responded to a few typical letters I've received from parents and look forward to answering many more. Please feel free to write to me of your concerns. I will always care. Finally, I've written a letter to parents seeking their understanding of the public school problems that teachers must face every working day. I believe that public schools can answer the needs of our children, but we must all care.

These letters are the musings of a writer, an educator, a patriot, and a parent who, like you, wants the best life has to offer for our children. I care.

Dear Adam,

The foster families passed you around, the teachers dreaded having you in their classes, and the EH teachers, struggling daily with your violent tantrums, hoped you would be absent. Who could blame them? You were impossible! I was a wide-eyed second-year teacher; you were an oversized, aggressive first grader, and I cared for you.

You kept looking for boundaries in your world. You pushed adults to their limits trying to force them to control you. You dared them to love you and terrorized the entire school with your temper. Each time you lashed out, it was as if you were responding to an attack that only you could see. I sensed the intense fear permeating your violent little being.

One day when you erupted into one of your typical, apparently unprovoked fits of rage, kicked over a desk, and threw a chair, the nurturer just budding in me reached out to the terrified, emotionally starved infant in you, and I did something I had never done before and have not done since. I picked you up and carried you out of the room. (No small feat, I might add.) While you fought me, I put both arms around you and held you tightly, saying, "I'm bigger than you are; I'm stronger. I will protect you. I *will* control you. You will not hurt yourself or other children because I won't allow it. You will follow rules in my class because I care for you." I repeated this several times, continuing to hold you until you calmed down. Your large eyes grew very wide as you studied me. Without a word you went back into the class, picked up the desk and chair, and decided to rest a moment before beginning assignments again. I'm not sure what you thought, but I know you held my hand often and hugged me every day before leaving school. We had a good year together.

Oh, Adam, why did you make all the years that followed so hard for yourself? Didn't you ever find the boundaries again? Maybe you just got too big for someone to hold.

Dear Dan,

Thank goodness your mother was finally convinced to move you from first grade to kindergarten. Yes, you were intellectually superior, but as an only child you had rarely played with other children. You were physically smaller than all of the other boys, and the thick, large, black-rimmed glasses added to your troubles with them. Those glasses simply wouldn't sit well on your tiny nose, and you spent a lot of time pushing them in position on that pale little face.

To be so small, you certainly were aggressive, dangerously aggressive. If something didn't suit you, you'd grab a pencil and attack another child. The counselor, your mother, the principal, and I worked together to help you. The aggressiveness lessened, but the immaturity remained. No matter how fast we may try to push her, Mother Nature most often demands that we have patience and spend time in the process of growing. After beginning kindergarten (the grade you had skipped), you calmed down, and as time passed, you began to work better with other children.

I saw your mother a few years ago. She said that you were doing well in school and had many friends. She believed that moving you back a grade had made all the difference. I agree.

I think of you those times when I try to rush my own growth. Your memory reminds me that maturing does not imply constant movement in one direction and that wisdom often counsels patience, even an occasional step back.

Many best wishes.

Dear Samantha,

Have you learned to use the pronoun *we?* It really won't do for you to use it as you did at age five. When you learned that *we* meant "two or more people," I don't think you quite understood. One day during recess, some boys tried to take your swing. They jerked on the chains trying to cause you to fall out. You warned them, "Leave me alone." They continued annoying you, and you repeated several times, "Leave me alone." As they became more aggressive about taking your swing, in desperation you bellowed, "If you don't leave me alone, I'm going to kick the hell out of *we!*" You kept your swing.

Samantha, I do hope you can use *we* correctly now, and thanks for the laugh!

Dear Mary,

Freckles and red hair, a gentle and quiet fourth grader. How I hurt for you when you were raped by a trusted, frequent visitor in your home. Will counseling and therapy ever help you overcome this trauma? Will the adults in your future be sensitive to your scars? I still think of you and the many days we talked of your fears; I remember your courage. I feel such rage that so much of your childhood was torn from you; that you had to learn so early that some trust is dangerous; that you had to spend so much time and energy healing when you should have been romping through childhood. You're a survivor. I need to believe that you'll lead a happy life. You are so deserving.

Dear Hank,

Yes, you were spanked. You were a healthy, mischievous, young man in sixth grade, much larger than all of the other students, and you reveled in that fact. You threatened them to and from school, and you made good those threats. You inflicted many bruises and instilled fear. Counseling, time-outs, changes in your schedule, and inducements to behave seemed of little consequence to you. After all else had failed and you were spanked, your behavior improved dramatically. Your parents' total lack of discipline had created an oversized monster. When you discovered that you could be controlled, you seemed to feel more comfortable. You began to show respect for authority figures and their requests. The other children, being forgiving by nature and relieved of the daily fear of your abuse, began to become your friends. Without developing some respect for authority, how could you have been able to function in an adult world with laws governing and restricting behavior? I lost track of you several years ago, but the last I heard you were playing basketball in high school and were only involved in occasional misbehaviors.

I'm glad for you that you were controlled as a child before the realities of the law came crashing down upon you in the world of adults.

Besides, isn't it nicer to be loved than feared?

Dear Marshall,

Anger can be all-consuming, becoming our only companion, robbing us of every other human emotion desperately needed to nourish our spirits. You see, a soul won't let itself be empty. It will store the anger we feed it. Yet, like the natural healing powers within our bodies, there is a drive within that urges us from defeat and despair to victory and survival. Your present anger can be a healthy defense against your pain. It will help you live through these terrible childhood days until a time when you can release the anger and fill your spirit with joy and forgiveness and go on with your life.

These were the words I wanted to say to you, but you were too young to understand. So I listened to your hurt and anger as you screamed and cried that your mother was a whore; as you told of the endless trail of men each evening in and out of your home; as you cried about the "uncles" who moved in, often abused you, and eventually disappeared.

Perhaps, all you needed then was for me to listen. But you're older now. Did you let the anger go? Did you find the peace and love you so desperately wanted? I hope so . . . I truly hope so.

Dear Allan,

Cigarette burns, beatings, and mental abuse . . . in and out of children's shelters . . . poor school grades . . . poor student relationships . . . poor teacher relationships . . . no friends . . . no love. This seemed to be the collage that made up your life. How I agonized each time the agencies placed you back into your home. Why did they do it? It was beyond my understanding, and I'm sure it was well beyond yours as you tried to live through each miserable day. I no longer have the tolerance needed to deal with these public agencies. My patience is used up, my endurance threadbare. I couldn't help you. You had become such a product of your stark, uncaring world that I couldn't even wish that I could take you home. I hope that one day you find love.

Dear Janice,

How many times did I ask, "Where are your glasses?" How many times did you respond with a broad, toothless six-year-old grin and frantically begin searching through your pockets and desk? There are some children whose personalities are tragically affected by physical handicaps, but not yours. Severely visually impaired, and diagnosed as having progressive visual deterioration until possible blindness, you merrily skipped into class each day, loving everyone and being loved by everyone. Together we worked to keep your glasses on your nose because you were usually so caught up in enjoying the moment that you absentmindedly laid them down. During the next few years your vision continued to deteriorate, but your spirit blossomed. You add to the world, Janice; your sight may be impaired, but your soul is unfettered. You're blessed, and we're blessed that you share yourself and remind us of the simple joy to be had in living each day.

Thank you, Janice, for being one of my teachers.

Dear Robby,

Setting the neighbor's utility room on fire, vandalizing your neighborhood, using drugs, alcohol, and cigarettes, and being arrested were, indeed, ambitious accomplishments for a fifth grader. What on earth are you doing now? Are our taxes supporting you in prison somewhere? You were a child I never reached. But how were you ever to become likeable when your mother said in your presence how much she hated you? She couldn't see that she was causing you to hate yourself, to destroy yourself. She turned down all offers of counseling services. I was left with one alternative—to survive you and your mother. I did, but my goodness, what became of you?

Dear Norwood,

You were the "Fraction King" of the fourth grade. We worked together to overcome your fear of math, your poor self-image, and your lack of confidence. By the end of the year you delighted us all by flexing your muscles in front of the room, declaring yourself the "Fraction King."

You'll never know the joy you gave me the day I ran into you at Penney's Department Store and you told me you were majoring in mathematics in college. Congratulations! "To life, Norwood!"

Dear Ellen,

I'm glad that you're all right. What timing! What a surprise! Swallowing a barrette the day the governor's wife visited our school certainly kept us on our toes!

I hope your tastes are becoming a bit more digestible.

Dear Sandy,

The circus performers at our school delighted all of the children, but you particularly liked the dog show. You laughed more than you had all year. Your battle with leukemia was a full-time job that didn't leave you much energy for joy. It was hard on us too. Though we prayed, your teachers and I, that you would win the physical war your body fought, we knew too well the prognosis for one so young. Your battles forced us to confront our own finitude, challenged our faith, outraged our sense of justice.

Thank you for rewarding me with a wonderful spontaneous smile when I took you backstage to pet the dogs and to meet the performers.

For me, administration was filled with so few rewards. Time had to be given to scheduling and planning, union matters, meetings, curriculum and staff development, conferences, staffings, noninstructional and instructional personnel, ad infinitum, but those few minutes I spent with you made it all worth it. Your smile blesses those who love you. In the midst of the demanding business of fighting leukemia, you found a moment of pure joy. Thank you for sharing it with me.

Dear Brian,

We tried, Brian. The psychologists, counselors, therapists, teachers, administrators, and your parents. Over a few years, you were serviced by SLD, Occupational Therapy, Counseling, and Speech. Many conferences, many staffings, and complete annual evaluations were devoted to your case, yet little improvement could be detected. You were socially withdrawn, and academics were difficult even though you were intellectually above "average." Complete physicals revealed no health problems that should have affected your ability to retain information. I imagine everyone felt as impotent as a surgeon with a dull scalpel. I know I did. Using all of our collective knowledge, we sought answers, but were left feeling hopelessly inadequate. You're blessed with caring parents who will continue trying throughout your lifetime. Perhaps, someday we'll have the answers for all children. I wish we could have served you better, Brian.

Dear Eric,

Of all the children I cared for and prayed for, you touched me most. I would have adopted you, if your mother had allowed it. At age five, you were beautiful, intellectually gifted, and had a mischievous twinkle that somehow managed to survive the physical and mental abuses inflicted at home.

Protective custody at HRS frustrated me practically to tears. Every time you came to school with the flesh on your face torn by your mother's fingernails, or a lump on your head from the bottle she used to hit you, or the bruises from beatings, I called HRS and pleaded with them to take you from the home. They told me they had been involved with your case for a long time. Probably irritated because my reported repetitions of your abuse reminded them of the failure of their rehabilitation efforts with your mother, they said that they would investigate again. In the meantime, she was killing your spirit and endangering your life. After the last time that I called HRS about you, your mother took you and left town. I'll probably never see you again, but you're in my thoughts—the little boy who had so much promise and such pain. Please live, Eric, survive—body and soul; keep your twinkle.

Dear Friends and Colleagues in the World's Noblest (not oldest) Profession,

I have shared your despair over the declining quality of product our schools have generated, your sad loss of pride in the title "Teacher," and your frustration at a world that somehow stopped demanding that we set high standards of performance and threatened legal action when we tried to impose them. Many of you absorbed all of this and did your best anyway; many quit trying and defined the profession as simply a joyless job. No one paid you or rewarded you for "dedication," yet everyone demanded it of you.

The multitudes of children from illiterate families who enter the public schools are relentlessly increasing. You are asked to prepare these children, who come through your doors already "academically and socially delayed," to meet the challenges of an advanced civilization. You are asked to address the varied individual needs of every handicapped and gifted child. You are asked to educate all children to their fullest potential in a day when many children are unable to discipline themselves for school-related tasks because the distractions which grab at them from all sides are more demanding and diverse than any generation of humans has ever known: from drugs to video games; from family distress to nuclear nightmares. Their concerns are for surviving the day rather than preparing for their futures.

Riding a technological tidal wave, you are attempting to educate a "star wars" generation. Alone, as you have largely been, the task is literally impossible. Major reform is hardly ever initiated from within. From Superintendent to Teacher, you spend most of every day dealing with immediate demands, paddling to keep your heads above water in a sea of daily crises. Even if you had taken the time and energy to strive for radical change, public support would not have been forthcoming.

But you are no longer alone. Education is becoming a major issue at the highest levels of government and the topic of conversation in every community. All over the nation, parent groups are forming to support educational reform. Ally yourselves with these groups. In the final analysis, it is only constructive community pressure and support that will restore the role of education to the prominence it must have for the sake of all our futures. With the support of our communities and with an attitude of immediate reform, we can shoulder these burdens together, accepting neither the blame for our "societal" ills nor the honor of "curing" those ills. We will share instead in the pride of seeing our children become productive and responsible American citizens. That's what we "signed on" to do in the first place.

This book then has been for you as well as parents. As more parents genuinely care about the quality of education and become involved with our schools, and as they begin to accept mutual responsibility for educating our nation's children, the profession of teaching will become better respected. In the next two decades we will either meet the needs for reform head-on or become useless, archaic relics of a scientific and technological space age. By the year 2000, we can have the public's respect once again if we include them in our efforts to overcome the urgent problems of the present. Writing this book represents my contribution to reform.

Sharing secrets of the system, I believe, may be the impetus needed to awaken the sense of need and suggest a constructive direction for parent involvement. We know that parents believe education does improve the quality of life, but they have lost faith in our abilities and the system's capacities to meet the demands of our times. We cannot blame them for losing faith; we have faltered ourselves a time or two. But the time is right, help is in sight, and success is realistically possible. Our country and our children need us now. Let's not fail them.

Terry

A FEW LETTERS FROM PARENTS

Dear Terry,

When I visited my son Larry's third grade class, I was shocked to discover that the teacher could not control twenty-five students. They stood on desks and crawled around the room as she yelled and they continued to disobey. She told me that this was a "bad class" and that she had been unable to control them all year. Do teachers sometimes have "bad classes"?

Irritated Father

Dear Irritated,

"Bad classes" are often teachers' excuses for lack of professional expertise. It seemed that during my eleven years in education each year the same teachers had the "bad classes" and others constantly had the "good classes." But regardless of whether or not this "bad class" is the fault of Larry's teachers, your child is being deprived of an adequate education because of the poor learning environment. There are several alternatives for action. I would advise that you consider writing a description of your visit. Take your written statement to the school's administrator and discuss the law in your state that pertains to this particular problem. For example, Florida law states in Chapter 6B-4.09, Criteria for Suspension and Dismissal, "1. (a) Inefficiency . . . (2) repeated failure on the part of a teacher to communicate with and relate to children in the classroom, to such an extent that pupils are deprived of minimum educational experiences . . ." Though punitive action against the teacher is probably not your goal, the fact that you are armed with your state's law will probably get the principal's attention. Perhaps you'll want to seriously discuss a new classroom assignment for Larry.

Terry

Dear Terry,

My child, Stephanie, is exceptionally intelligent, but we are unable to afford the "extras." We would like her to be able to take music, art, and language lessons. Any suggestions?

Stephanie's Mom

Dear Stephanie's Mom,

Our nation is fortunate to have many wonderful volunteers. Utilizing resources such as city libraries, churches, service organizations, or school and county volunteer organizations, communities are able to provide a variety of services. Piano, art, and language lessons may be attainable through one of these sources. A little research can help you find that special person.

Terry

Dear Terry,

My son's kindergarten teacher wants to let him skip kindergarten and move to first grade. I'm confused. What do you recommend?

Confused Mother

Dear Confused,

Kindergarten provides many readiness skills in preparation for a demanding first grade reading, writing, and math curriculum. The teacher probably has evidence that your son has achieved these readiness skills, but there are many considerations other than academics. Physical, social, and emotional maturity, chronological age, and mental age need to be evaluated. The long-range picture should also be included as a serious criterion upon which to base your decision. Do you believe your son will want to be involved in athletic competition in school? If so, physical size, neuromuscular maturity, chronological age, grade, and emotional development will play an important role in his success. In many cases a child's entire school career and his lifetime attitudes about his relative abilities can be affected by whether he is constantly in the lower half of a grade level struggling to keep up with the average and superior performer (academics, sports, social skills, leadership, emotional maturity) or whether, because he is older than most, his skills, mind, and body are more refined and often advanced as compared to his schoolmates. All things being equal, if I were asked if I would rather have my child be the youngest in a class or the oldest, I would choose the latter, until an obvious need for change arose.

An appointment with a group of professionals such as the teacher, guidance counselor, curriculum specialist, and principal will add to your data for a better decision. If academics are the only concern, perhaps the kindergarten teacher(s) could provide a more challenging curriculum for your son or permit him to attend first grade for a few of his academic needs on a trial basis before you make a final decision. If you move him up a grade and the decision sours, it will predictably be much more painful to move him back again.

Terry

Dear Parents,

We teachers seek your understanding. We combat the system's problems daily. We know that reform must occur, and we are willing to fight on the front lines for that goal. But as in every battle, there must be support behind the "foot soldiers." We desperately need your support.

We want to teach in a climate of renewal where excellence and extra effort are respected and rewarded; where school boards courageously fight literally any battle to keep their best people and conscientiously work to filter out those who are unqualified to teach our children; where discipline is encouraged by the support and cooperation of parents and administrators; where parents demand quality course content and quality instruction; where parents teach their children to strive for excellence and self-discipline characterized by well-established family/community values; and where students accept the responsibility and value of becoming educated.

A rebirth of educational quality is long overdue. The overpowering problems of the system as it struggles to survive each societal crisis are suffocating. Out of our intense frustration some of us have left our profession to pursue other interests in our lives, but we're still concerned about our colleagues, the children, and their families.

It is our America, our children's, and their children's that is at risk. One day, we hope others who come to share our dreams of teaching as a respected and dignified profession may say, "We teach. Proudly, we teach in America, a strong nation, whose citizens are dedicated to individual and national excellence."

Best to each of you,
Teachers who need your support

MOVING FORWARD ...

I've told you some secrets, suggested some skills, given some information, and shared with you some of my most poignant memories of what this book is really all about—the children. We are ready for the next and final chapter, which takes our last step. It addresses the need to improve the "stuff" the schools currently offer and explains how we parents can improve that "stuff."

Permit me to share one last personal experience to illustrate the need for all of us to take a closer look at our local schools. A young man attending a Georgia high school outside of Atlanta graduated in the top 5 percent of his class. He had taken all advanced high school offerings and made A's and B's in those courses. Yet he couldn't score well enough on the SAT, a college entrance examination, to qualify for the college of his choice.

He claimed that A's in high school were easy and required little or no study. Through perseverance he managed to be accepted probationally into a fine university, but he is struggling with demanding courses requiring well-defined study habits. This is a serious, responsible young man who took the "most challenging" courses offered in high school and was inadequately prepared to cope with college. His parents were misled to believe that he was progressing well because his grades in courses with impressive sounding titles like Algebra II were good. They all received a psychological blow inflicted by a system that promised something it didn't deliver. (Promise: If your child does well in elementary school and high school, he will predictably be prepared for college.)

Let's take a look at how something like this could have occurred.

10
Who Speaks for the Children?

Throughout this book I have played variations on one consistent theme: Even a moderately sized public school system is a complex organizational network, a ponderous, plodding dinosaur that, however well intentioned, must concern itself with the problems of managing the many and, therefore, is not likely to be able to render maximum advocacy for any individual child. It is possible for the needs of the individual to be submerged in the concerns of the many. For that reason, *if you want your child to gain maximum advantage of the public school system, you must see to it! You must assume the role of an EP-A/R.* And I have emphasized that the most effective way to deal with the individuals who daily affect the life of your child is through *diplomacy, not aggression.*

It is wonderful that you care enough to take parenting seriously. Relatively speaking, your decision to be an EP-A/R puts you far above the crowd. But, there is more. The great sea turtle pulls herself laboriously upon the beach, digs a hole, and lays a hundred or so eggs in the sand. She covers the eggs carefully and disappears once more into the waves. The little ones will hatch in good time and make their way alone toward the water. The birds will get most of them before they reach their destination; the predators of the sea will get many of the rest before they mature enough to defend themselves. But the balance of nature will have been served. There will be just enough turtles in the sea and most of those will be strong and healthy. Their mother did her job by placing them in the world; natural selection did the rest. The mother bird nurtures her young still further until they can fly and hunt for themselves. The natural logic of human parenting is not so merciful to the parents. We bear them, rear them, and provide them with the tools for fulfillment, but even when they leave the nest, we never relinquish a deep concern for their well-being. We have the additional responsibility of doing all we can to provide a climate in which they have the maximum opportunity to use the tools we have given them. It is to that issue that we must now address ourselves.

"A NATION AT RISK"

As never before in the history of our country, the probabilities for optimism concerning our future are considerably less than are the occasions for pride in our past.

In August 1981, Secretary of Education Terrell Bell created the National Commission on Excellence in Education, directing it to examine the quality of American education. This commission was composed of outstanding leaders in the field of education and the community at large. Eighteen months later, they submitted their report and entitled it "A Nation at Risk." The title itself reflects the general tone of this report. On the very first page the commission expresses its concerns in even stronger language: "If an unfriendly foreign power had attempted to impose on America the mediocre educational performance that exists today, we might well have viewed it as an act of war." With minimal reservations,

I find myself in passionate agreement with the findings, the recommendations, and the title of this report. It examined the products of our educational system relative to our past and relative to that of other industrialized nations. The following are only a few of their discoveries, but they faithfully represent the general trend.

Indicators of the risk:

• International comparisons of student achievement, completed a decade ago, reveal that on 19 academic tests American students were never first or second and, in comparison with other industrialized nations, were last seven times.

• Some 23 million American adults are functionally illiterate by the simplest tests of everyday reading, writing, and comprehension.

• About 13 percent of all 17-year-olds in the United States can be considered functionally illiterate. Functional illiteracy among minority youth may run as high as 40 percent.

• Average achievement of high school students on most standardized tests is now lower than it was 26 years ago when Sputnik was launched.

• Over half the population of gifted students do not match their tested ability with comparable achievement in school.

• The College Board's Scholastic Aptitude Tests (SAT) demonstrate a virtually unbroken decline from 1963 to 1980. Average verbal scores fell over 50 points and average mathematics scores dropped nearly 40 points.

• College Board achievement tests also reveal consistent declines in recent years in such subjects as physics and English.

• Both the number and proportion of students demonstrating superior achievement on the SAT's (i.e., those with scores of 650 or higher) have dramatically declined.

• Many 17-year-olds do not possess the "higher order" intellectual skills we should expect of them. Nearly 40 percent cannot draw inferences from written material; only one-fifth can write a persuasive essay; and only one-third can solve a mathematics problem requiring several steps.

• There was a steady decline in science achievement scores of U.S. 17-year-olds as measured by national assessments of science in 1969, 1973, and 1977.

• Between 1975 and 1980, remedial mathematics courses in public 4-year colleges increased by 72 percent and now constitute one-quarter of all mathematics courses taught in those institutions.

• Average tested achievement of students graduating from college is also lower.

• Business and military leaders complain that they are required to spend millions of dollars on costly remedial education and training programs in such basic skills as reading, writing, spelling, and computation. The Department of the Navy, for example, reported to the Commission that one-quarter of its recent recruits cannot read at the ninth grade level, the minimum needed simply to understand written safety instructions. Without remedial work they cannot even begin, much less complete, the sophisticated training essential in much of the modern military.

With much more similar data in hand, the Commission perceived patterns that allowed for some general grouping of the data. "We conclude that declines in educational performance are in large part the result of disturbing inadequacies in the way the educational process itself is often conducted. The findings that follow, culled from a much more extensive list, reflect four important aspects of the educational process: content, expectations, time, and teaching."

Content

What are we teaching in our schools, and are we keeping our curricula current with the vast increase of knowledge and technology? In order to answer this question, the Commission compared the patterns of courses taken in high school in

230 / Secrets Parents Should Know About Public Schools

1964–1969 and those typically taken in 1976–1981. Their conclusion was, "Secondary school curricula have been homogenized, diluted, and diffused to the point that they no longer have a central purpose. In effect we have a cafeteria-style curriculum in which the appetizers and desserts can easily be mistaken for the main courses."

In the past, students tended to direct their efforts toward either college preparatory courses or vocationally oriented ones; between 1964 and 1979, however, there has been an increase from 12 percent to 42 percent of students electing a shapeless path toward graduation called "general track." The major theme of this track seems to be extensive opportunity for student choice. "Twenty-five percent of the credits earned by general track high school students are in physical and health education, work experience outside the school, remedial English and mathematics, and personal service and development courses, such as training for adulthood and marriage." In thirteen states, 50 percent or more of the units required for high school graduation may be electives chosen by the students.

Psychologists agree that one of the fundamental characteristics of adolescence is the tendency to grab short-term pleasures at the expense of long-range goals. And so in our inexplicable wisdom we have prescribed fewer and fewer courses which they must take and given them more and more options. Given this freedom, it is certainly not surprising that increasing numbers of our students choose courses such as "bachelor living" instead of calculus regardless of what their predictable future needs might be.

All of this is further confounded by the fact that satisfactory completion of all units necessary for graduation makes absolutely no universally accepted statement as to the level of education attained. For example, Florida has recently instituted a Functional Literacy Test as a criterion for graduation from its high schools because successful completion of the course work is not in itself a guarantee of this achievement.

Expectations

How do we define priority and importance in terms of the level of knowledge, abilities, and skills high school and college graduates are expected to possess? How much time, effort, self-discipline, and motivation are required to meet our definition of "high student achievement"? In each of the areas examined to determine answers to these questions, notable deficiencies were discovered.

- The amount of *homework* for high school seniors has *decreased* (two-thirds report less than one hour a night), and *grades* have *risen* as average student *achievement* has been *declining.*"
- "In many other industrialized nations, courses in mathematics (other than arithmetic or general mathematics), biology, chemistry, physics, and geography start in grade 6 and are required of *all* students. The time spent on these subjects, based on class hours, is about three times that spent by even the most science-oriented U.S. students, i.e., those who select 4 years of science and mathematics in secondary school."
- High school diploma requirements are ludicrous and reflect no consensus as to reasonable expectations.
- Minimum competency examinations (now required in thirty-seven states) fall far short of what is needed to function in an increasingly sophisticated world or to pass college core courses. These minimum scores tend to become the standard as fewer and fewer achieve or exceed them; thus, the educational standards are lowered for all.
- "One-fifth of all 4-year public colleges in the United States must accept every high school graduate within the State regardless of program followed or grades, thereby serving notice to high school students that they can expect to attend college even if they do not follow a demanding course of study in high school or perform well."
- "About 23 percent of our most selective colleges report

that their general level of selectivity declined during the '70s, and 29 percent reported reducing the number of specific high school courses required for admission." They could not continue to be as selective as in the past and have enough students to keep their doors open.

• Textbooks are being "written down" to the ever-lower reading levels in response to perceived market demands. These books do not challenge the better students at all.

• Expenditures for textbooks and other instructional materials have declined by 50 percent over the past seventeen years.

Time

In weighing the evidence presented to it, the Commission identified three major concerns about how our schools and students utilize time: "(1) as compared to other nations, American students spend much less time on school work; (2) time spent in the classroom and on homework is often used ineffectively; and (3) schools are not doing enough to help students develop either the study skills required to use time well or the willingness to spend more time on school work."

• In England and other industrialized countries, it is not unusual for academic high school students to spend 8 hours a day at school, 220 days per year. In the United States, by contrast, the typical school day lasts 6 hours and the school year is 180 days.

• In many schools, the time spent learning how to cook and drive counts as much toward a high school diploma as the time spent studying mathematics, English, chemistry, U.S. history, or biology.

• A study of the school week in the United States found that some schools provided students only 17 hours of academic instruction during the week, and the average school provided about 22.

• A California study of individual classrooms found that because of poor management of classroom time, some elementary students received only one-fifth of the instruction others received in reading comprehension. [Note: This evidence reinforces the parents' need to use ITM skills discussed in Chapter 7.]

• In most schools, the teaching of study skills is haphazard and unplanned. Consequently, many students complete high school and enter college without disciplined and systematic study habits.

Teaching

"The Commission found that not enough of the academically able students are being attracted to teaching; that teacher preparation programs need substantial improvement; that the professional working life of teachers is on the whole unacceptable; and that a serious shortage of teachers exists in key fields."

In professional literature in which critics can afford to be less diplomatic than can the members of a national commission, the criticism of the trends in the teaching profession is scathing. Former U.S. Commissioner of Education Sterling M. McMurrin wrote, "It is a national scandal that large numbers of teachers are inadequately prepared in the subject matter they teach as well as in the elements of a genuinely liberal education. This is, in my view, the major weakness of American education."

There is a general "buck passing" among those involved as to where the real blame for our educational malaise lies. The remedy most often suggested for poor student performance is smaller classes. In response, "President Johnson of Fisk University once commented, 'Keeping classes small by staffing them with mediocre teachers merely enables them to transmit their mediocrity in an intimate environment.' "

Concern over the adequacy of teacher education and ability is not simply fabricated by those needing to deflect blame from themselves. In the Houston, Texas, school district, half of those applying to be teachers had lower scores on a math achievement test than did the average high school junior, and a third of them were defective in their ability to use the English language. In 1983, the legislators in both Florida and Arizona found it necessary to pass laws requiring that teacher applicants pass a literacy test.

Former Assistant Superintendent of Schools for New York City Francis Griffith minces no words as he deplores the pressures which have made a mockery of the teaching profession in that city. On the subject of present teacher education, he denounces the disparity between the number of methods courses and the number of content courses prospective teachers are required to take. "Those who elect to become teachers," he asserts, "elect themselves out of a broad general education." Lest he be perceived as being objectively dispassionate on the subject, he continues,

> The teaching profession has become a refuge for second-raters and those looking for a lifetime position from which they cannot be dislodged even for glaring incompetence, thanks to spineless administrators and teachers' unions. The philosophy of academic egalitarianism which grants access to higher education to all, regardless of past achievement, makes it possible for dullards and misfits to enter teaching. This is not to deny that there are men and women teaching in our schools who are first-rate in every way and whose commitment to young people is genuine. There are many such but their number is diminishing and their replacements are usually a lesser breed.

> Teachers constitute the nation's largest profession. The impression that they are academically superior to the average college graduate is unsupported by evidence. Thousands were themselves mediocre students. The ablest college graduates generally do not enter teaching.

While the general public may not have gathered specific data by which to support its conclusions, a recent Gallup Poll leaves no uncertainty that society's image of the teaching profession has diminished. To the question "Would you like to have a child of yours take up teaching in the public schools as a career?" only 45 percent responded yes in 1983 as compared to 75 percent in 1969. It is unclear what may be all of the causes for such a response, but the negative trend seems obvious.

Indeed, teachers are part of the problem, but let's not hang all of the ills of the system on their collective and convenient necks. Political pressures forced lowered standards for teacher selection, and colleges of education, needing to keep up enrollment, lowered entrance and course requirements. Prospective eagles often complain of enduring required courses that are virtually devoid of relevant, meaningful content.

Decline in Other Areas of American Society

For the past several years the Gallup Poll has shown that the American public believed that lack of discipline was the biggest problem faced in our schools. The problems of lowered standards are compounded by the lack of discipline. We have fewer teachers prepared to deal with more difficult discipline problems than our country has ever confronted. The sixties and seventies spawned dangerously permissive attitudes which delivered into the classrooms of the eighties hostile youths with a general disdain for any authority figure, while at the same time diminishing the power of school personnel to deal with the problems they created.

Educational leaders, also caught up in the spirit of the times, developed equally permissive philosophies. During one of the years that I taught in an open-space school, a master teacher told me that I expected too much of my fifth grade students because I required all work to be well written (complete sentences, proper paragraph structures, etc.). She commented that this would "stifle their creativity."

John Goodlad, one of the most highly respected educational thinkers and researchers of our time, writes on the first page of his latest work, *A Place Called School: Prospects for the Future,*

> American schools are in trouble. In fact, the problems of schooling are of such crippling proportions that many schools may not survive. It is possible that our entire public education system is nearing collapse. We will continue to have schools, no doubt, but the basis of their support and their relationship to families, communities, and states could be quite different from what we have known.

And, indeed, 5.6 million families who can afford it have already placed their children in private institutions.

Seeking to involve the general public in immediate remedial action, the Commission asserts that the national interest is directly related to the quality of the education of our youth.

> Another dimension of the public's support offers the prospect of constructive reform. The best term to characterize it may simply be the honorable word "patriotism." Citizens know intuitively what some of the best economists have shown in their research, that education is one of the chief engines of a society's material well-being. They know, too, that education is the common bond of a pluralistic society and helps tie us to other cultures around the globe. Citizens also know in their bones that the safety of the United States depends principally on the wit, skill, and spirit of a self-confident people, today and tomorrow. It is, therefore, essential—especially in a period of long-term decline in educational achievement—for government at all

levels to affirm its responsibility for nurturing the Nation's intellectual capital.

And perhaps most important, citizens know and believe that the meaning of America to the rest of the world must be something better than it seems to many today. Americans like to think of this Nation as the preeminent country for generating the great ideas and material benefits for all mankind. The citizen is dismayed at a steady 15-year decline in industrial productivity, as one great American industry after another falls to world competition. The citizen wants the country to act on the belief, expressed in our hearings and by the large majority in the Gallup Poll, that education should be at the top of the Nation's agenda.

It was not included in their original charge that the Commission should comment beyond the scope of the educational factors which they claim place the nation at risk. But, our charge as parents is more complex. However disquieting, perhaps we should seek to examine a bit more extensively the America of the past quarter-century.

If we have for one moment a doubt that, indeed, America is at risk, this furtive backward glance should put it firmly to rest.

  • Though both major political parties decry the practice of deficit spending, claiming that it is destructive to the nation, each as it gains control of the government vigorously participates in it and irresponsibly spends money, plunging the nation even deeper into debt. Chanting, "Reelection above all," each party strives to cause the efforts of the other to fail so as to affect the public choices in the next election. America loses—no one wins, certainly no one's children.
  • We sought to solve our energy problems by becoming dependent for our oil upon the most volatile area on the face of the planet and by grabbing the nuclear tiger without firmly legislating an absolute mandate for safely han-

dling its waste. We created windfall profits taxes that tend to discourage initiative and financial creativity and a federal income tax system that encourages devious loophole-finding. We designed a welfare system which entices the poor to become permanently dependent. Labor unions, once the salvation of the American worker, spend much of their efforts protecting incompetence and nurturing shoddy workmanship.

• Between 1972 and 1982, violent crime in our country increased 54 percent. When we do apprehend criminals, we seem unsure of what to do with them. The public confidence in the court system is at the lowest ebb ever.

• At the expense of thousands of young Americans, we involved ourselves for many years in two wars which we did not try to win.

• Perhaps the greatest obscenity of all is that in order to preserve our peace of mind, we have insulated ourselves from the panic and rage that the knowledge of these travesties should naturally produce; the cost of this insulation is an immobilizing sense of passivity and impotence. Can such a scenario be interpreted in any other way than descriptive of a social order falling apart?

Is it a coincidence that this apparent irrational and self-destructive behavior of our people and our leaders represents a breakdown of the same values which lie at the very core of excellence in education: adequate data gathering, rational organizing of the data, examining the full logical consequences of each possible alternative use of the data, and, finally, bold decisiveness in choosing the alternative most likely to be beneficial? What will be the outcome of such folly?

Whatever causal relationship may exist between the decline in our educational product and these other areas of national distress is too complex to prove. They are parallel, and they undoubtedly have some relationship. Both are clearly related to the changes in values and practices which are detrimental to all of our citizens.

REFORM

The good news is, both educational and social decline can be reversed! Reform in education can lead in the long run to reform in our country. The great American philosopher and educational innovator John Dewey taught that the clue to overcoming personal and social ills is to alter a society's habits, its habits of response and of thought. Nothing is more important than education in remodeling a society. Because we are creatures of habit, *education can provide the conditions for developing the most useful and creative habits.*

Although the nation mumbles about many of the social ills referred to earlier and some organized efforts are being made to attack most of them, the general public, though increasingly more conservative in its political position, does not seem to be very excited about any one attempt at social reform. On the other hand, there is a rising tide of concern about the plight of public education. In response to the Commission's findings, many parent groups are becoming active, and school leaders are riding the crest of this interest to improve conditions within their schools. And that brings us back to you, dedicated, caring parents.

Of all the great minds which our nation has produced, none has characterized the spirit of America more than Will James. James believed that the human organism was at its best when it was passionately involved in and committed to achieving a desired goal. Ironically, he discovered that war universally caused the species to put aside trivia, place full attention to the task at hand, and most efficiently channel its energies to achieve. Yet, "War," he said, "is immoral. Our task is to discover *the moral equivalent of war.*" Maybe we've finally done it; the perceived threat to a nation's youth is the closest possible experience to war, and its eradication represents the highest morality of the natural order. What is more primitively logical than that nurturing, protective parents should instinctively take up the gauntlet when they are convinced that their offspring are in real and present danger?

EPCAR: The Parent's War on Educational Mediocrity

"What," you exclaim, "after all these pages and my laborious efforts to master all of these skills, after I have finally become a graduate EP-A/R, you're telling me that that's not enough?"

That's right. It is unavoidably apparent that the existing system is inadequate to provide a substantial educational base for many of America's youth. It also seems clear that whatever loss of values has caused its decline, a parallel diminishment of principles is running unchecked through our society in general. If the world in which your child will mature is going to be a healthy, happy, and productive place, no one is more likely to be motivated to provide it than you. As always in our great country, the impetus for change begins where it should, with concerned people; the people make our institutions responsive! That's part of the legacy of freedom. Challenges are a rich part of the joy and excitement of life. We are at our finest as we passionately involve ourselves in responding to them.

Therefore, I encourage you to extend your relationship to the public school system beyond the EP-A/R role and include another dimension that I call "EPCAR" (Educational Planners and Child Advocate-Representatives), groups for educational excellence. I coined this term to show a natural extension from the nurturing and protective aspect of parenting, to that of the provider who inspects the terrain ahead concerned with the future safety and sustenance of her offspring.

At the end of its report, The National Commission on Excellence in Education addresses you, our nation's parents, and identifies a task that I invite EPCAR parents to elect as a first step in reversing the downward trend in education.

To Parents
You know that you cannot confidently launch your children into today's world unless they are of strong character and well-educated in the use of language, science, and mathematics. They must possess a deep respect for intelligence, achievement, and learning, and the skills needed to use them; for setting goals; and for disciplined work. That respect must be accompanied by an intolerance for the shoddy and second-rate masquerading as "good enough."

You have the right to demand for your children the best our schools and colleges can provide. Your vigilance and your refusal to be satisfied with less than the best are the imperative first step. But your right to a proper education for your children carries a double responsibility. As surely as you are your child's first and most influential teacher, your child's ideas about education and its significance begin with you. You must be a *living* example of what you expect your children to honor and to emulate. Moreover, you bear a responsibility to participate actively in your child's education. You should encourage more diligent study and discourage satisfaction with mediocrity and the attitude that says "let it slide"; monitor your child's study; encourage good study habits; encourage your child to take more demanding rather than less demanding courses; nurture your child's curiosity, creativity, and confidence; *and be an active participant in the work of the schools.* Above all, exhibit a commitment to continued learning in your own life. Finally, help your children understand that excellence in education cannot be achieved without intellectual and moral integrity coupled with hard work and commitment. Children will look to their parents and teachers as models of such virtues.

Talk with other parents about your convictions, and you will discover that you are not alone in your willingness to become involved. Many parent groups are already actively working for excellence in our schools under the auspices of official parent-teacher organizations and other unofficial but influential parent groups. Given the opportunity and seeing concerted efforts, many school people will eagerly become devoted partners with you in raising standards of performance, in encouraging a renewed respect for mind, a compassion tempered by the awareness of consequences, and a sense of personal discipline related to achievement. They will willingly share with you the task of promoting the values of respect for one's self, respect for the rights of others, and a spirit of patriotism.

Seek, and you will surely find support from our political leadership. Education has become a "hot potato." In the Gallup Poll of 1980, 80 percent of those asked stated that they believed schools were "extremely important" to one's future success, and over half of the respondents affirmed their willingness to pay more taxes to improve our educational standards.

President Reagan addressed the nation in April 1983, responding to the report of the Commission. He acknowledged the seriousness of their findings and revealed plans to implement many of their recommendations. He addressed you: "Parents, please demand these and other reforms in your local schools, and hold your local officials accountable. Let our parents once again be the rudder that puts American education back on course to its success through excellence." Then he committed himself:

We've sent to the Congress a tuition tax credit plan, and proposed a voucher system to help lower and middle income families afford the schools of their choice. We've proposed education savings accounts to help families save for college education. We've sent legislation to the Congress that would create block grants for the training of math and science teachers, and another proposal would encourage those teachers to keep abreast of new developments in their fields.

We've also begun an effort to honor some of our finest math and science teachers. For the sake of all our children, our country, and our future, we must join together in a national campaign to restore excellence in American education. At home, in school, in state government and at the federal level, we must make sure we have put our children first and that their education is a top priority.

"Train up a child in the way he should go," Solomon wrote, "and when he is old he will not depart from it." Well, that's the God-given responsibility of each parent and the trust of every child. It is a compact between generations we must be sure to keep.

The war on educational mediocrity can be won if we pull together. To begin the campaign, I suggest the following steps.

1. Use the information in this book to become an involved, enlightened EP-A/R, and encourage your friends to do the same. Helping one child at a time succeed, using the best the system currently offers, is top priority until its destructive deficiencies are remedied.

2. Take the initiative to explore the possibilities of beginning an active EPCAR group within your community.

3. Help shape the direction of the efforts of your group by reviewing, adapting and implementing all possible and appropriate recommendations made by the Commission. Though your child may currently be in elementary school, become active in high school reform now because it will take a few years for reform to take place.

RECOMMENDATIONS OF THE NATIONAL COMMISSION ON EXCELLENCE IN EDUCATION

Following is a brief summary of the Commission's recommendations. The complete report is much more specific, and your group may want several copies.

Recommendation A: Content

We recommend that State and local high school graduation requirements be strengthened and that, *at a minimum, all* students seeking a diploma be required to lay the foundations in the Five New Basics by taking the following curriculum during their 4 years of high school: (a) 4 years of English; (b) 3 years of mathematics; (c) 3 years of science; (d) 3 years of social studies; and (e) one-half year of computer science. For the college bound, 2 years of foreign language in high school are strongly recommended in addition to those taken earlier.

Whatever the student's educational or work objectives, knowledge of the New Basics is the foundation of success for the after-school years, and, therefore, forms the core of the modern curriculum. A high level of shared education in these Basics, together with work in the fine and performing arts and foreign languages, constitutes the mind and spirit of our culture.

Recommendation B: Standards and Expectations

We recommend that schools, colleges, and universities adopt more rigorous and measurable standards, and higher expectations, for academic performance and student conduct, and that 4-year colleges and universities raise their requirements for admission. This will help students do their best educationally with challenging materials in an environment that supports learning and authentic accomplishment.

Recommendation C: Time

We recommend that significantly more time be devoted to learning the New Basics. This will require more effective use of the existing school day, a longer school day, or a lengthened school year.

Recommendation D: Teaching

This recommendation consists of seven parts. Each is intended to improve the preparation of teachers or to make teaching a more rewarding and respected profession. Each of the seven stands on its own and should not be considered solely as an implementing recommendation.

1. Persons preparing to teach should be required to meet high educational standards, to demonstrate an aptitude for teaching, and to demonstrate competence in an academic discipline. Colleges and universities offering teacher preparation programs should be judged by how well their graduates meet these criteria.

2. Salaries for the teaching profession should be increased and should be professionally competitive, market-sensitive, and performance-based. Salary, promotion, tenure, and retention decisions should be tied to an effective evaluation system that includes peer review so that superior teachers can be rewarded, average ones encouraged, and poor ones either improved or terminated.

3. School boards should adopt an 11-month contract for teachers. This would ensure time for curriculum and professional development, programs for students with special needs, and a more adequate level of teacher compensation.

4. School boards, administrators, and teachers should cooperate to develop career ladders for teachers that distinguish among the beginning instructor, the experienced teacher, and the master teacher.

5. Substantial nonschool personnel resources should be employed to help solve the immediate problem of the shortage of mathematics and science teachers. Qualified

individuals including recent graduates with mathematics and science degrees, graduate students, and industrial and retired scientists could, with appropriate preparation, immediately begin teaching in these fields. A number of our leading science centers have the capacity to begin educating and retraining teachers immediately. Other areas of critical teacher need, such as English, must also be addressed.

6. Incentives, such as grants and loans, should be made available to attract outstanding students to the teaching profession, particularly in those areas of critical shortage.

7. Master teachers should be involved in designing teacher preparation programs and in supervising teachers during their probationary years.

Recommendation E: Leadership and Fiscal Support
We recommend that citizens across the Nation hold educators and elected officials responsible for providing the leadership necessary to achieve these reforms, and that citizens provide the fiscal support and stability required to bring about the reforms we propose.

To obtain copies of the entire report, see page 252 of the Bibliography. *A Place Called School,* by John Goodlad, is also worth your consideration.

As you have read, most of the findings and recommendations from the Commission are concerned with the "products" of the system: high school and college students. Most of you who read this book are parents of children in elementary school, where the foundations are laid. You will, of course, need to translate the recommendations, where appropriate, to the school attended by your child. Obviously, the distempers of learning that characterize the findings of the Commission began much earlier than high school and the values which produced them are deeply embedded within the whole educational system.

EP-A/R GOAL: AS AN EP-A/R, ENSURE THAT YOUR CHILD GAINS MAXIMUM ADVANTAGE FROM THE PRESENT SYSTEM OF PUBLIC EDUCATION.

EPCAR GOAL: AS AN EPCAR, DEMAND A CLIMATE OF EDUCATIONAL EXCELLENCE IN OUR COUNTRY FOR ALL OF OUR CHILDREN AND FOR THE PROTECTION OF OUR NATION.

▶ Skill: *Dedication* to your child's academic progress and future.

▷ Secret: (Well, not so much of one when you consider our proud tradition.) TOGETHER, AMERICANS CAN DO IT!

RESULT:

The result is beyond price. Our children will be prepared to meet the challenges of adulthood with the knowledge, skills, and attitudes necessary to succeed, and the world into which they emerge will be a compatible one, ready to reward them for their efforts and their ingenuity. This is the substance of the American Dream and the legacy of effective parenting.

P.S. to Amy,

Knowing how deeply conscientious you are causes me to fear that you may believe that the information in this book places an overwhelming burden upon you as a caring parent. It was not written with that intent, I assure you. I'm keenly aware of the tremendous amount of time and energy you spend caring for three young children and your husband, and working each day. You're busier now than you ever have been or probably ever will be. That is why I've tried to share secrets and pinpoint time-saving EP-A/R skills that will help you take preventative measures now to save precious time and prevent problems in the future.

We can promote EPCAR within the limits of our daily schedules. We can try to involve our friends whose children are in college; they may have more time. We can share our thoughts with middle-aged and retired people; many of them will have the time, skill, "know-how," and community influence to take leadership roles. We don't have to do it alone. At the very least, together our families can be committed to educational excellence as a daily emphasis in our communities and in our homes.

Your loving sister,
Terry

A Selected
Bibliography

A Report to the Nation and the Secretary of Education by the National Commission on Excellence in Education. "A Nation at Risk: The Imperative for Educational Reform," *American Education*, 19 (June 1983), 2-3, 5-17.

ABC Television Special. "To Save Our Schools: To Save Our Children." September 1984.

Anonymous. "On the Education Front," *Parade Magazine*, January 15, 1984, p. 13.

Barber, Larry W., and Karen Klein. "Merit Pay and Teacher Evaluation," *Phi Delta Kappan*, 65 (December 1983), 247-51.

Becker, Henry Jay, and Joyce L. Epstein. "Parent Involvement: A Survey of Teacher Practice," *The Elementary School Journal*, 83 (November 1982), 85-102.

Black, Theodore M. *Straight Talk About American Education*. New York: Harcourt Brace Jovanovich, 1982.

Bluestein, Jane. "Grand Plan for Classroom Management," *Instructor*, 93 (September 1983), 74-77.

Boehm, Ann E. *The Parents' Handbook on School Testing*. New York: Teacher's College Press, 1982.

Bogdan, Robert. "P.L. 94-142—A Closer Look at Mainstreaming," *Educational Forum*, 47 (Summer 1983), 425-34.

Brophy, Jere E. "Classroom Organization and Management," *Elementary School Journal*, 83 (March 1983), 265-85.

Caldwell, Janet H., William G. Huitt, and Anne O. Graeber. "Time Spent in Learning: Implications for Research," *The Elementary School Journal*, Illinois: The University of Chicago Press, 82 (May 1982), 471–80. (Research for Better Schools, Inc. Philadelphia, Pennsylvania.)

Chandler, Harry N. "Title I and Learning Disabilities: The Creatures from the Federal Swamp," *Journal of Learning Disabilities*, 15 (March 1982), 183–85.

Chandler, Harry N., and Karen Jones. "Learning Disabled or Emotionally Disturbed: Does It Make Any Difference? Part 1," *Journal of Learning Disabilities*, 16 (Aug.–Sept. 1983), 432–34.

Clark, David L., and others. "The Changing Structure of Federal Education Policy in the 1980's," *Phi Delta Kappan*, 65 (November 1983), 188–93.

Culyer, Richard. "Chapter I Programs: Problems and Promising Solutions," *Clearing House*, 57 (January 1984), 231–38.

Dillon, Linda, and Malcolm Brown. "Quality Circles: Tools for Assessing Effectiveness and Planning Strategies," *NASSP Bulletin*, 67 (October 1983), 50–53.

Elam, Stanley M. "The Gallup Education Surveys: Impressions of a Poll Watcher," *Phi Delta Kappan*, 65 (September 1983), 26–32.

Flesch, Rudolf Franz. *Why Johnny Still Can't Read*. New York: Harper & Row, 1981.

Florida Teacher Competencies, Concepts and Ideas. "Relationships Between Florida Competencies and Effective Teaching Domains," 1983.

Fraser, Barry J., and Darrell L. Fisher. "Use of Actual and Preferred Classroom Environment Scales in Person-Environment Fit Research," *Journal of Educational Psychology*, 75 (April 1983), 303–13.

Friedman, Paul G. *Communicating in Conferences*. Illinois: ERIC Clearinghouse on Reading and Communication Skills, 1980.

Frinks, Marshall L. Handouts on "The Education Consolidation and Improvement Act of 1981," *State of Florida Department of Education* (August 1981).

Gallup, George H. "The 15th Annual Gallup Poll of the Public's Attitudes Toward the Public Schools," *Phi Delta Kappan*, 65 (September 1983), 33–47.

Goodlad, John I. *A Place Called School: Prospects for the Future*. New York: McGraw-Hill, 1983.

Goodlad, John I. "Teaching: An Endangered Profession," *Teachers' College Record*, 84 (September 1983), 575–78.

Goodlad, John I. "What Some Schools and Classrooms Teach," *Educational Leadership*, 40 (April 1983), 8–19.

Graham, Patricia Albjerg. "The Twentieth Century Fund Task Force Report on Federal Elementary and Secondary Education Policy," *Phi Delta Kappan*, 65 (September 1983), 19–21.

Griffith, Francis. "Teachers Are Part of the Problem," *American Education*, 19 (October 1983), 12–15, 18.

Hastings, Anne H. "Snipping the Strings: Local and State Administrators Discuss Chapter 2," *Phi Delta Kappan*, 65 (November 1983), 194–98.

Hawkins, Robert B., Jr. "Current Crises in Public Education," *American Education*, 19 (April 1983), 30–34.

Hill, Napoleon, and E. Harold Keown. *Succeed and Grow Rich Through Persuasion*. New York: Ballantine Books, 1982.

Hoffman, Michael S. "The Quality of Education Can Be Improved," *NASSP Bulletin*, 67 (December 1983), 70–72.

Kirk, Samuel A., and James J. Gallagher. *Educating Exceptional Children*, 3d ed. Boston: Houghton Mifflin Company, 1979.

Knight, Michael E. *Teaching Children to Love Themselves*. Englewood Cliffs, N.J.: Prentice-Hall, 1982.

Kuntz, Susan W., and Richard Lyczak. "Sustained Efforts of Title I over the Summer Months," *Journal of Educational Research*, 76 (Jan.–Feb. 1983), 148–52.

Lieberman, Myron. "Teacher Bargaining: An Autopsy," *Phi Delta Kappan*, 63 (December 1981), 231–34.

Mann, Lester, and others. "LD or not LD, That Was the Question: A Retrospective Analysis of Child Service Demonstration Centers' Compliance with the Federal Definition of Learning Disabilities," *Journal of Learning Disabilities*, 16 (January 1983), 14–17.

Massee, Bernard. "Quality Control in Education," *Clearing House*, 57 (October 1983), 66–68.

Peterson, Penelope L., and Susan R. Swing. "Beyond Time on Task: Students' Reports of Their Thought Processes During Classroom Instruction," *The Elementary School Journal*, 82 (May 1982), 481–91.

President Reagan's Radio Address to the Nation of April 30, 1983, Houston, Texas. "The President's Radio Address to the Nation on Education," *American Education*, United States Department of Education, 19 (June 1983), 4–5.

Purkey, Stewart C., and Marshall S. Smith. "Effective Schools," *The Elementary School Journal*, 83 (March 1983), 427–52.

Sametz, Lynn, and Caven McLoughlin. "Teachers' Knowledge of the

Law As It Affects Children: Technical Note," *Perceptual and Motor Skills*, 56 (April 1983), 565–66.

Soar, Robert S. "Teacher Evaluation: A Critique of Currently Used Methods," *Phi Delta Kappan*, 65 (December 1983), 239–46.

Staub, Susan E. "Compulsory Unionism and the Demise of Education," *Phi Delta Kappan*, 63 (December 1981), 235–36.

Vance, Grant W. "Statistics of the Month," *American Education*, 19 (Jan.–Feb. 1983).

Weinstock, Ruth, "A Title I Tale: High Reading/Math Gains at Low Cost in Kansas City, Kansas," *Phi Delta Kappan*, 65 (May 1984), 632–34.

Weiser, Margaret G. "The Right to Be a Child," *Childhood Education*, 59 (Jan.–Feb. 1983), 146–50.

Winn, Wynona, and Alfred P. Wilson. "The Affect and Effect of Ability Grouping," *Contemporary Education*, 54 (Winter 1983), 119–25.

Wynne, Edward A. *Looking at Schools: Good, Bad, and Indifferent.* Lexington, Mass.: D.C. Heath & Company, 1980.

Zahorik, John A. "A Test on Teaching," *Clearing House*, 57 (February 1984), 245–47.

Ziomek, Robert L. and William Schoenenberger. "The Relationship of Title I Student Achievement to Program and School Attendance." *Elementary School Journal*, 84 (Nov. 1983), 232–40.

DOCUMENTS AVAILABLE BY MAIL ORDER
Report by the National Commission on Excellence in Education entitled "A Nation at Risk: The Imperative for Educational Reform."
Address:
ERIC Document Reproduction Service
3900 Wheeler Ave.
Alexandria, Virginia 22304
Include: $5.65 plus shipping
Request: The title and #226006, a paper copy

Other copies may be obtained in bookstores nationwide or from:
USA Research
Consumer Publications
812 Memorial Drive, Suite 1802
Cambridge, Massachusetts 02139
617-354-1200

The cost is $5.95 in paperback and $10.95 in hardback. To cover handling and shipping please add $1.00 per order plus .50 per copy. Send check, money order, or account number for VISA or MasterCard, noting the expiration date on your credit card. Indicate the name and address, including zip code, to which the order should be shipped and provide your telephone number.

The 15th Annual Gallup Survey of Public Attitudes Toward Public Schools.
Address:
    Phi Delta Kappan
    P.O. Box 789
    Bloomington, IN 47402
Minimum order: 25 copies for $7.50
Additional copies: 20 cents each

National Education Association Leaflet Assortment provides information for parents.
Address:
    NEA Professional Library
    P.O. Box 509
    West Haven, CT 06516
Request: Stock No. 5100-9-10
Cost: $5.95